Bright Ideas
Assemblies

Written by Helen Banks

Contents

Published by Scholastic Publications Ltd,
Marlborough House, Holly Walk,
Leamington Spa, Warwickshire CV32 4LS.

© 1987 Scholastic Publications Ltd

Reprinted 1988

Some ideas drawn from Scholastic
magazines.
Written by Helen Banks
Edited by Sue Quilliam
Illustrations by Chris Saunderson

Printed in Great Britain by
Loxley Brothers Ltd, Sheffield

ISBN 0 590 70693 4

Front and back cover: Martyn Chillmaid
Hannukiah supplied by H Becher
Diva supplied by R Kanwar

4 INTRODUCTION

6 OURSELVES
The same, but different 7
Special things 8
Seeing 9
It's tasty 10
Language 11
Bookworm 12
Look what I have learnt to
 do 13
Feelings 14
Fears 15
Who rules – OK! 17
Linda's lie 18
Helping hands 19
The growth of inequality 20
Patience is a virtue 21

22 FAMILY AND FRIENDS
This is your life 23
Family life 24
Weddings 26
A new baby 27
Mothering Sunday 28
Nan, Grandad and Pop 29
Best friends 30
Next-door neighbours 31

Your own Coronation
 Street 31
Moving on 32

34 LIVING WITH OTHER PEOPLE
New things 35
What's your hobby? 36
Superpeople 37
Brave people 38
When I needed a neighbour 39
Turning the other cheek 40
Sharing 41
Compassion 42
Mind your manners 43
Co-operation 44
Responsibility and caring 46
Joe Homan's Boys' Town 47

48 THE ENVIRONMENT
The cycle of life 49
Homes 50
Feeding the birds 51
Busy bees 52
Down on the farm 53
Water is life 54
Dinosaurs and all that rubbish 55
Animals in danger 56

Signs around us   58
'I spy' on my way to
   school   59

60   HEALTH AND SAFETY
Road safety   61
Warnings   62
Firework safety   63
Recipe for life   64
You are what you eat   65
The opening door   66
First Aid   68
Health for all   69

70   INTERESTING EVENTS
TV-am   71
Space exploration   72
The mayor's visit   73
The school outing   73
The marathon   74
A Victorian school day   75
The Children of Courage
   awards   76
The building of the Bell Rock
   lighthouse   77
Market day   78
Tomorrow's world   79

80   STORIES FROM DIFFERENT CULTURES AND RELIGIONS
The family of man and
   woman   81

Story-tellers   81
Texts from world religions   82
In the beginning – an African
   tale   83
Dreamtime   84
Confucius and friends   85
The sign of Sikhism   86
The story of Mahagiri   87
Games around the world   88
The wounded swan   90
The dove with the olive
   leaf   90
The mouse and the crow   91

92   ROUND THE YEAR
The year ahead   93
Valentine's Day   94
Spring growth   94
All Fool's Day   95
May Day   96
World Children's Day   97
St Swithin's Day   98
Back from the holidays   99
A bumper harvest   100
Hallowe'en   101
Remembrance Sunday   102
Winter   103

104   FESTIVALS
Eid-ul-Fitr   105
Carnival time   105
Chinese New Year   106

Pancake Day   107
Pesach: the feast of the
   Passover   108
Holi   109
Palm Sunday   110
Easter poles   110
New light, new life   111
Diwali   112
Advent   113
An advent ring   113
An advent calendar   113
Happy Christmas   114
Christmas around the
   world   115

116   REPRODUCIBLE MATERIAL
Assemblies Calendar   122
Useful addresses   124
Keys to songbooks and prayer
   books   126
Acknowledgements   127

Introduction

No book on assemblies is tailor-made for every school – by their nature, school assemblies reflect the total environment; the size of the school, the age of the children, their background and interests. The aim of this book is to provide a wide range of topics and styles of presentation, which you can modify or expand to suit the needs of your own particular school.

If children are to understand and learn from assemblies, it is important that the assemblies should be relevant to their lives and be made as enjoyable and interesting as possible. Assemblies are a community experience and, as such, should reflect the wider community. So there is room for Christian, multi-faith and secular assemblies.

Some of the assemblies in the book are designed to be presented by the teacher alone. However, most involve the children to some extent, and some are intended for class presentation. Like all good teaching, assemblies require a degree of preparation and the following are some factors to consider when adapting ideas to suit your own situation.

Abbreviations for prayer and song books are used throughout the book. The full titles are given on page 126. Teachers will undoubtedly already have their favourites, and the one's given in this book are suggestions only.

HOW TO INVOLVE CHILDREN
The principle that children learn by doing is just as important in assemblies as it is for the rest of the primary school curriculum. Involve children as much as possible, whether directly, in some form of activity, or through their responses to ideas presented in the assembly. However, this should not preclude some time and space for quiet reflection – assemblies can provide a peaceful break from the otherwise hectic schedule typical of most primary schools.

USING YOUR OWN STRENGTHS
The way that teachers present assemblies is as individual as their classroom styles. However, a school assembly is a more exposed situation, so make the most of your own strengths. If you enjoy being in the limelight, exploit the opportunity. If you prefer to work from behind the scenes, encourage your children to take the lead. Whatever your talents – use them!

SIZE OF ASSEMBLY
The number of children and the spread of age groups involved will influence the way you choose to present a topic. The age range suggested for each of the assembly ideas provides a rough guide, but judge for yourself whether an idea suits your age group or not. It is usually easier to achieve an informal exchange of ideas in a smaller group. The larger the assembly, the more explicit the structure required. Whatever the size, always take into account the range of interests, abilities and experience of your audience.

ORGANISATION
The way you choose to seat the children will affect the formality or informality of the occasion. Many schools now adopt a semi-circular arrangement with the presenter in the middle. This helps everyone to feel involved. Whether or not the teacher chooses to sit or stand also influences her/his relationship with the children. Similarly, the use of a stage or blocks can help children to focus on the teacher and others involved, but can also have a distancing effect. When organising your assembly, decide which effects you wish to achieve.

4

USING A THEME

It is often helpful to link assemblies by a theme, allowing time to explore ideas in greater depth, and incorporating a wider range of experience. This approach can also help teachers to prepare for and follow up ideas in their own classrooms.

TIMING

This is impossible to prescribe, since it depends so much on the children's ability to concentrate – something we all know varies from day to day. In general, it is best to keep assemblies short, and to take into account the time children have already spent sitting whilst everyone enters the hall.

VISUAL PROPS

The use of posters, slides, symbols, labels, real objects, etc greatly helps to focus the children's attention, and to highlight points being made in an assembly. Children are growing up in a visually orientated world, and are therefore more responsive to visual communication. Visual supports are more likely to guarantee that a message will not be forgotten.

DRAMA

Assemblies are essentially a form of performance or drama, so it's best to capitalize on this. This does not mean that every assembly should be a major production, but the children's improvisations can greatly enhance an idea.

MUSIC

The music selected for an assembly can significantly affect the mood. It can be calming, uplifting or positively riotous – so make sure you know which effect you require and when.

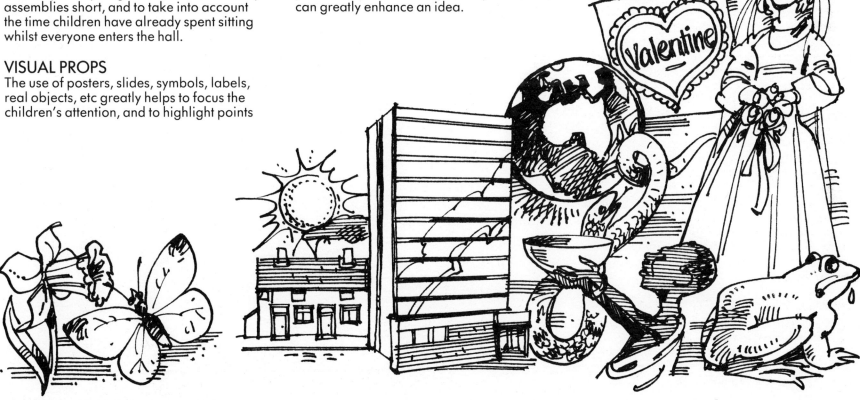

Ourselves

The same, but different

Age range
Five to nine.

Presentation
Teacher (and class).

What you need
Story *Tusk, Tusk*, David McKee, Anderson/Hutchinson.
Prayers *LBCP*, pages 34, 35.
Songs 'The Ink is Black, the Page is White', *SSL*; 'Think of a World Without any Flowers', *SSL*; 'The Family of Man',*CP*.

What to do
Split your class into pairs. This needs to be done with care and awareness of possible areas of distress for children. Ask each pair to think about their appearance; their families, friends, homes and interests. On the basis of this they make two lists — one for things that are the same for both of them and the other for things that are different. During the assembly select some of your pairs and ask the other children if they can spot any similarities and differences. The pair can then report on their own findings.

Tell the children about a class of children in another country — choose a country that you know something about. Ask the children what similarities/differences they think there would be between those children and themselves.

Read the story *Tusk, Tusk*. This tells of a group of black elephants and a group of white ones who hate each other. The groups fight each other until only a few peace-loving elephants are left alive. These disappear into the jungle until, some years later, some grey elephants emerge. These live harmoniously together until the ones with big ears and the ones with little ears start giving each other strange looks.

Special things

Age range
Five to eleven.

Presentation
Teacher.

What you need
A collection of your own personal treasures – souvenirs, heirlooms, old toys, your children's first attempts at drawing etc.

What to do
Explain to the children that you are going to show them some of your own special treasures. One at a time, show them the treasures and talk about why they are special to you, how you came to get them, how long you have had them and any interesting stories that go with them. Point out that they need not be expensive or beautiful to be special and that all of them mean a great deal to you.

Ask the children if they have any similar treasures of their own. Where do they keep their treasures and do they let other people touch them? Maybe some of them have a treasure hidden on them at that moment – a good time to spot all those stickers, model figures and other toys sneaked into assembly! Tell the children how important it is to respect other people's possessions, no matter how small, inexpensive or battered they are, since one can't always tell how important these may be to their owner.

Seeing

Age range
Five to twelve.

Presentation
Teacher.

What you need
A blindfold; a bag containing some objects to be recognised by touch; examples of Braille and other information available from The Press Officer, Royal National Institute for the Blind, 224 Great Portland Street, London W1.
Prayer *LPT*, page 18.
Hymn 'He Gave Me Eyes so I Could See', *SSL*.

What to do
Play a short game of 'I spy' with the children. Talk about how they had to use their eyes to look for clues. Blindfold a volunteer and ask him or her to try to identify an object from the bag by using their hands. A few more children can then have a turn. Explain that blind people have to make clever use of their senses of touch and hearing. Blindfold another child and ask him or her to listen very carefully to see how many sounds he or she can identify.

Tell the children about Louis Braille. Louis became blind when he was three years old so he knew something about the things around him that he could no longer see. He wished that he could read books like other people and when he grew up he worked hard to invent a special alphabet that blind people could use. He made an alphabet in which the letters are raised above the surface. Show the children the examples of Braille.

The RNIB also have all kinds of inventions to help blind people, such as a liquid level indicator which bleeps when a cup or jug is full, a wristwatch which opens to enable you to feel the hands and a football which makes a noise.

It's tasty

Age range
Five to eight.

Presentation
Teacher and some children.

What you need
A variety of foods for children to identify through tasting.
Make some very easy (eg crisps and chocolate) and
some more difficult. Include rice, grain, powdered milk
and dried biscuits.
Prayer *LBCP*, pages 84, 85.
Song 'Push the Trolley', *NH*.

What to do
Select a group of children as volunteer tasters. Blindfold
a few at a time and ask them to identify some of the
foods. Ask them to try to describe the texture as well as
the taste. Talk about the variety of foods available in our
Western shops and supermarkets. What are the
children's favourite tastes? Draw attention to the fact that
in many countries there is little or no choice.

Language

Age range
Eight to twelve.

Presentation
Teacher.

What you need
Examples of sign language from the Royal National Institute for the Deaf, pencil and paper, greetings in different languages displayed on large pieces of paper (see pages 123 and 124).

What to do
Start by telling the children that you are going to teach them how to greet each other in several languages. Use the display cards to teach them the greetings. Although we spend much of our time talking, there are other ways that we can send messages. For instance, we can write messages or draw pictures. Ask for some volunteers – give one group of children some written messages which they must translate into a pictorial message eg 'Go and fetch a book', 'Clap your hands', 'Sit down on the floor'. They then hand their message to one of the children in the other group to see if he or she can understand it. Explain that people who are born deaf find it very difficult to learn to talk because they cannot hear sounds but they can learn to 'talk' with their hands. Demonstrate some examples of sign language.

Through our actions we send messages to other people. Shake your fist at the children – what does this mean? Stamp your foot – what does this tell them? Invite the children to come and demonstrate sad, happy, angry, bored, excited, surprised and tired expressions and actions.

Conclude by showing the children that even if you don't speak the same language as someone else there are other ways of communicating – often a smile is enough.

11

Bookworms

Age range
Seven to twelve.

Presentation
Teacher and class.

What you need
Photocopies of the Bookworm sheet, on page 117.
Song 'The Ink is Black, the Page is White', *SSL*.

What to do
You will need to do some preparation work in the classroom prior to the assembly. Split the class into groups of three or four. Each group has to select three books that they have all enjoyed reading. Encourage them to select a variety of styles – poetry, humour, adventure etc. For each book they complete a Bookworm worksheet describing what the book is like and why they enjoyed it. Then ask the groups to complete the following sentence with as many ideas as they can think of: 'A good book is . . .'. Finally, each group makes up a short play or puppet show based on a selection from one of their books.

Let the children present some of their work in the assembly – Children's Book Week in October would be a good time to choose to do this. Emphasise that reading can be a pleasurable activity, both when alone and when shared with others.

Look what I have learnt to do

Age range
Five to twelve.

Presentation
Teacher.

What you need
Prayer *LBCP*, page 58.

What to do
This assembly can be held as a one-off or may develop into a weekly event. Ask each class teacher to nominate a child who has learnt or done something special that week; for example, how to write their name, a forward roll or an exciting story. Make sure that you know the children's names and exactly what they have done, as demonstration of their skills may require resources such as a PE mat or paint and paper.

During the assembly, ask the children to come to the front to talk about and demonstrate their new skills. How do they feel about their achievements? Who helped them to learn their new skills? What do they aim to learn to do next?

This assembly is particularly helpful in a large primary school, since it allows the children a glimpse of what the other children are doing at different ages and provides a chance to appreciate the needs and aspirations of other people.

Feelings

Age range
Five to twelve.

Presentation
Teacher.

What you need
Poems: Your own selection of poems describing feelings.
For example: 'Happiness', A A Milne, in *Rhyme Time*,
Hamlyn/Beaver; 'The Quarrel', E Farjeon, in *A First Book
of Poetry*, Oxford; 'Loneliness', Pomroy, in *Junior Voices
1*, Penguin; 'Anger', Lowe, in *Junior Voices 1*, Penguin.
Prayer *LPT*, pages 28, 29, 37, 41.

What to do
Everyone has feelings, although they are not things that
you can see, smell or touch. Ask the children to think of
some 'feeling' words – happy, sad, hurt, frightened,
excited, anxious etc. Sometimes you can tell what people
are feeling by their expressions and what they say or do.

Ask for some volunteers. Give each child, or pair of
children, a card describing a particular situation and the
feelings aroused by it. Whisper this information to
younger children. Examples of situations and feelings
could be: you have discovered that your ticket to
Saturday's football match is missing from your pocket;
your Mum has brought home a kitten to be your very own
pet; someone has knocked over the model you have just
finished. Ask the volunteers to act out each situation, and
see if the other children can tell how they are feeling.

Explain to the children that you may not be able to
touch feelings with your hands, but people can touch your
feelings with their words or behaviour. Talk about some
of the things people say or do that hurt other people's
feelings. How can we help people to feel better?

Now read some of the poems that you have selected.
Ask the children to think about things that affect their
feelings and to watch how the things that they do and say
affect other people's feelings.

As a follow-up activity, the children could complete the
photocopiable worksheet on page 118.

Fears

Age range
Five to eight.

Presentation
Teacher.

What you need
A set of 'ink blot' pictures, made by dropping black paint onto a large sheet of paper which is then folded in half.
Prayer *TWI* 22.
Song 'I Whistle a Happy Tune', *AP3*.
Stories *There's a Nightmare in my Cupboard*, Mercer Mayer, J M Dent & Sons Ltd, 1976; *Long Neck and Thunderfoot*, Michael Foreman, Puffin.

What to do
Show the children the 'ink blot' pictures and ask them what they can see or imagine in the pictures – strange creatures, monsters, faces etc. Explain that in the dark we sometimes look at quite ordinary objects and can imagine that they are something completely different.

Read *There's a Nightmare in my Cupboard*. A little boy imagines that there is a nightmare in his cupboard and one night he decides to get rid of it once and for all. He finds that it is not that frightening after all and the nightmare is even afraid of him. He is therefore able to come to terms with his bedtime fears.

Tell the children about your own childhood fears and encourage them to share their own. Explain that we are often frightened of things because we don't know what they are and that sharing your fears can help you to understand them.

15

Who rules – OK!

Age range
Eight to twelve.

Presentation
Teacher and class.

What you need
Poem see page 17.
Prayers *LBCP*, pages 58, 59.
Song 'This Way, That A-Way', OK.

What to do
Before the assembly read the poem to your class. Discuss who exactly was making the rules! School rules are not usually written down but are an agreed code of behaviour. Split your class into groups and get them to agree on some school rules which they think would make the school a better place to work and play. Pool their ideas and get the children to illustrate each of their rules.

Once more in groups, get the children to invent a game and make sure that the rules are quite clear and that everyone has agreed on them. See if the children can explain the rules of the game to their friends. What happens if anyone breaks the rules? Does this have anything to do with disagreements on the playground?

Introduce the assembly by reading the poem *Supply Teacher*. Ask the children why we need rules. Can people live together without rules? The class can present their 'school rules' and explain why they think they need them. They could also talk about the rules of their invented games.

Explain that all religions provide rules or codes for conduct. The following quotes show that there is a theme which connects most religions.

'Do unto others as you would that they should do unto you' (Christian); 'Do unto all men as you would wish to have done unto you' (Muslim); 'Do nothing unto others which you would not have done unto yourself' (Buddhist); 'What we do not wish others to do to us, may we not do unto others' (Sufi).

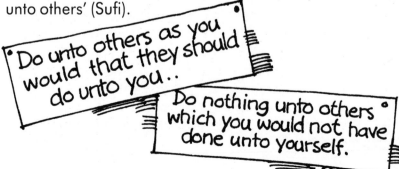

Supply teacher

Here is the rule for what to do
Whenever your teacher has the flu,
Or for some other reason takes to her bed
And a different teacher comes instead.

When this visiting teacher hangs up her hat,
Writes the date on the board, does this or that;
Always remember, you must say this:
'*Our* teacher never does that, Miss!'

When you want to change places or wander about,
Or feel like getting the guinea pig out,
Never forget, the message is this:
'*Our* teacher always lets us, Miss!'

Then, when your teacher returns next day
And complains about the paint or clay,
Remember these words, you just say this:
'The *other* teacher told us to, Miss!'

Allan Ahlberg

Linda's lie

Age range
Seven to twelve.

Presentation
Teacher.

What you need
Story 'Linda's Lie', *Dinner Ladies Don't Count*, Bernard Ashley, Puffin.

What to do
Stories or extracts often provide a good basis for an assembly. In this story Linda's parents are unable to afford the outing money for her class ballet trip but, rather than admit this to her teacher, Linda tells a lie. It is just a little lie, but she is horrified to see how it grows. The story sensitively explores her growing sense of guilt and discomfort having told a lie and the difficulties she encounters in trying to resolve the situation. The story shows that we can sometimes tell a lie for what seems a perfectly sound reason but that the consequences are then completely out of our control.

Helping hands

Age range
Five to eight.

Presentation
Teacher and involving all the children.

What you need
Language Resources, Bright Ideas Teacher Handbooks, Scholastic Publications — a source of finger rhymes. Songs 'Hands to Work and Feet to Run', *SSL*; 'Jesus's Hands are Kind Hands', *SSL*; 'He's Got the Whole World in His Hands', *CP*.

What to do
This is a good assembly to hold near the beginning of the Autumn term to give new children a sense of belonging. Before the assembly, ask each teacher to arrange for the children in their class to draw round, cut out and decorate a hand pattern. These also need to be named, ready for the children to bring them into the assembly. Pin frieze paper round the hall at a height which the children can reach.

As the children come into the assembly make a point of helping them and guiding them with your hands. See if they noticed what you were doing. Ask them to think of times when they have used their hands to help other people — taking someone's hand to show them the way; pointing to something; picking someone up when they have fallen over etc. Explain that in school we like to use our hands to help each other — to show that we wish to be friends with someone or to help each other at work.

One class at a time, with the help of its teacher, goes and sticks its hand patterns side by side round the frieze until everyone's hands are joined together. Whilst the teachers are helping the children to do this, the rest of the children can sing songs about hands or you could teach the children some finger rhymes and games.

The growth of inequality

Age range
Eight to twelve.

Presentation
Teacher.

What you need
Examples of seeds, beans, cress etc that the children have been growing; two large sheets of card with the following descriptive terms clearly printed on them.

What to do
Show the children the seeds that are growing. Talk about the correct conditions for growth – soil, darkness, light, water, warmth. Mention the problem of weeds. Why do we need to stop weeds growing among crops?

Illustrate that we can choose to become different sorts of people. Divide children into two groups and give each group one of the cards printed with the words that describe opposites. Comment on how both the groups are growing and developing as people. Ask the questions: If only one group existed in our school, what sort of place would it be to live in? How can our school become the sort of place we'd like? Draw the moral that each of us can choose the sort of person we want to be.

Healthy diet
Exercise
Practice
Clean
Tries
Curious
Friendly
Kind
Caring
Shares . Loves . Prays

Finicky
Lazy
Idle
Dirty
Careless
Tired
Bully
Cheat
Steals
Hates . Mean
Swears

Patience is a virtue

Age range
Seven to twelve.

Presentation
Teacher.

What you need
Prayers *CPAW* 33; *WYP* 176.
Songs 'Stick on a Smile', *ECS*; 'One More Step', *CP*.

What to do
Tell the story of Corrie ten Boom who was determined to make the best of things even in appalling circumstances. Use this to lead on to an assembly discussion about giving up too soon when things seem to be going wrong. Ask the children for examples and be prepared to join in with examples of your own, for example, a baby, when learning to walk, keeps falling down, but perseveres. Great pianists have often wanted to give up practising just like children! Talk about making the best of things rather than complaining when things don't go quite as hoped.

Corrie ten Boom (1892–1983)
During World War Two, Corrie ten Boom and her sister, Betsie, ran a watchmaker's shop in Holland. In it they courageously hid Jewish people who were being hunted by Nazi soldiers.

One day the Nazis found out what Corrie and Betsie were doing and arrested them. They were put in prison and then sent to a terrible concentration camp where they suffered much cruelty. Corrie's most treasured possession was a Bible which she managed to smuggle into the camp. She read it to the other prisoners and talked to them about Jesus, helping them to be patient and to keep cheerful. (Betsie died in the camp, but Corrie survived the war and eventually returned to Holland.)

21

Family and friends

This is your life

Age range
Seven to twelve.

Presentation
Teacher and people associated with the 'celebrity'.

What you need
Prayer *LPT 26*; *WYP* 167, 174.
Songs 'What is Your Name?'; *NO*, 'Everybody's Building', *CP*.

What to do
A member of the school could be chosen as the subject of a 'This is Your Life' sequence. Select someone with an interesting background: a person who was born in another country, perhaps, or whose parents or grandparents were born abroad. Pictures of places associated with them (the country of their birth, the street where they live, the school they attended etc) can be displayed following research by your class group. This could be the first in a series of assemblies, based on finding out about our schoolfriends, which deal with a representative from a different aspect of school life each week (pupil, teacher, secretary, cook etc).

Present the assembly on the lines of the TV programme and, if possible, include some surprises for the person concerned – perhaps a taped message from a distant relative.

Family life

Age range
Seven to twelve.

Presentation
Teacher.

What you need
Tape-recording of sounds in the daily life of one family – crunching breakfast cereal, starting the car, watching TV etc; information on patterns of living in other countries available from The Commonwealth Institute, Kensington High Street, London W8.
Prayer *LBCP*, pages 28, 29.
Songs 'The Family of Man', *CP*; 'Shelter Makes the Home and the Family', *NW*.

What to do
Family life varies enormously. Within your own school children will come from a range of backgrounds – single parent, foster home, the extended family etc. It is therefore best to focus on the variety that exists, extending this to patterns of family life in other parts of the world.

Start by playing the children the tape-recording of 'family sounds'. Ask them to identify what is happening and use this to draw on their own particular experiences of family life. Tell the children about family life in other countries.

Family life in Lesotho

The land in much of Lesotho is poor and it is difficult for families to grow enough to live on. Sometimes the men have to move to South Africa to find work and they then spend most of the year away from their families. This means that the women have to take all the responsibility for bringing up their children, looking after older relatives and also growing what few crops they can. Children grow up hardly knowing their fathers.

Life on a kibbutz

A kibbutz is a special sort of community that has been developed in Israel. Everyone lives and works together. Kibbutzim (the plural) are usually farming communities, although some now have factories. The parents share a variety of jobs, either working on the farm or doing household work. Everyone gets the same wage whatever work they do. The children are looked after in the school or nursery while their parents are working. The nursery will look after children soon after they are born. Everyone eats together at mealtimes; special times are set aside each day when children can be with just their parents.

Weddings

Age range
Five to nine.

Presentation
Teacher and children.

What you need
A wedding photo album, some children dressed in their 'wedding' outfits.
Music Wedding March, Mendelssohn
Story *When Willy Went to the Wedding*, Judith Kerr, Picture Lion.

What to do
In the classroom, ask the children to tell you about weddings that they have attended – hopefully you will hear about a variety of ceremonies – church, registry office, Christian, Muslim, Jewish etc. Use the children's ideas to produce some art work and written accounts of the weddings. These could be framed with doilies or gold paper to make them look special.

In the assembly the children can present their work and model their own special outfits.

Talk about the importance of the event to all the people involved and explain that they usually like to keep a record of the event in a special photo album.

Read the story 'When Willy Went to the Wedding' in which the appearance of all Willy's pets adds a bit of excitement to his sister's wedding day.

A new baby

Age range
Five to eight.

Presentation
Teacher.

What you need
A mother willing to bring a young baby into school. Baby accessories, baby bath, toys etc.
Story *A Baby Sister for Frances*, Russell Hoban, Hippo 1983.

What to do
Through dialogue between the mother and the class, explore the wonder of having a new baby in the family and how the baby's routine and needs affect everyone. Focus on how the baby changes as he/she grows up. Involve the children in relating their own experiences with babies and younger brother and sisters.

Read *A Baby Sister for Frances*. The story deals with feelings of jealousy over a new baby. Frances decides to run away, packs her belongings and goes and hides under the dining room table. Her parents acknowledge her feelings and through their sensitive handling of the situation help her to realise that she also has a unique role to play in the family.

Mothering Sunday

Age range
Five to twelve.

Presentation
Teacher and children.

What you need
'Supermum', Sandra Kerr.

What to do
Mothering Sunday falls on the fourth Sunday in Lent. It originates from the pagan festival which was held at this time of year when people worshipped a goddess called Cybele, who was known as the Great Mother of the gods.

On Mothering Sunday children thank their mother, usually by giving her a gift and a card. Violets and simnel cake were the traditional presents.

Although parents are often welcomed to assembly in schools, this is an obvious chance to invite mums and grannies. Read 'Supermum' and the children can read their own poems about mums and improvise scenes from family life that show all that a mum does.

You could have a quiz in the assembly for children and guests, hold up pictures of famous women and ask who is their son or daughter and vice versa.

The climax of the assembly comes when each child presents his or her mother with a cake or posy and a card which he or she made. Watch out for children whose mother was unable to be present.

28

Supermum
Who's stronger than a lion, gentle as a lamb,
Funnier than Chaplin, wise as Solomon?
Who flies around like lightning and never goes to bed?
It's Supermum, the wonderworker: kills all known germs dead.

> Supermum, you're wonderful, but very underpaid.
> Supermum, you're cook and cleaner, handyman and maid.
> If you put in a bill for all the work you do,
> There'd be an awful lot of wages due.

She's as generous as Robin Hood and all his Merry Men.
She's as kind as Florence Nightingale and then as kind again.
Like Superman, she's X-ray vision (she can see through me),
With a voice to rival Tarzan's when she calls us in for tea.

> Supermum, you're wonderful . . .

She's more wonderful than Wonderwoman, really quite a gal,
More honest and clean-living than Batman and his pal.
Her bark is just like Lassie's, far worse than any bite.
(A sharp word from our mum could give Count Dracula a fright.)

> Supermum, you're wonderful . . .

She could be made Prime Minister, she'd be superb at that;
She could be Queen of England, but she'd never wear a hat.
She should be made World President, she's sensible and good;
She'd keep those super powers in line if anybody could.

> Supermum, you're wonderful . . .

Nan, Grandad and Pop

Age range
Five to eight.

Presentation
Teacher and a group of children.

What you need
Prayer *LPT*, page 33.
Story *A Special Swap*,
Sally Wittman,
Scholastic Publications, 1980.

What to do
Arrange for a group of children to paint a picture and write a description of a grandparent or an old person that they know. The children introduce the assembly by presenting their work. Talk about the different special names that we have for grandparents, eg Nanny, Gran, Poppa, Grandad Fuller etc.

Ask the children how old people have to be before we think of them as 'old'. What happens to some people as they get older? At this point you could show the children a collection of pictures of people of all ages and ask them to pick out people they consider to be old. Explain that not all old people become ill or have difficulty walking but that most people slow down as they get older and need more time to do things. Invite the children to describe a time when they have been able to help an older person.

Now read *A Special Swap*. The story is about Old Bartholomew and his neighbour, little Nelly. They were great friends and their neighbours called them 'ham and eggs' because they were always together. When Nelly was small, Bartholomew pushed her in her pram, taught her to skate, and helped her when she really needed it. As Nelly got older, Bartholomew was the one who needed a helping hand – especially when he had an accident and had to stay in a wheelchair. Then it was Nelly's turn to take him for walks, and Bartholomew's turn to sit – a very special kind of swap.

Best friends

Age range
Five to eight.

Presentation
Teacher.

What you need
Prayers *TAP* 55; *LBCP* 34.
Songs 'Thank You for my Friends', *TB*; 'The Ink is Black, the Page is White', *SSL*.
Story *Best Friends for Frances*, Russell Hoban, Hippo.

What to do
Ask the children to think carefully about all the times that they have played and worked with their friends over the last few days – at home, in the playground, in school. Select children to come and talk about their friends and why they like them. Can they remember how they first made friends? How do they show their friends that they like them? Perhaps they can think of some words to describe the qualities of a good friend.

Read the story *Best Friends for Frances*. This is an amusing tale of how Frances establishes friendships and expresses the need of all children to feel accepted.

Next door neighbours

Age range
Seven to twelve.

Presentation
Teacher and class.

What you need
Hymn 'Think, Think on These Things', *SSL*.
Prayer *LBCP* 34.

What to do
Children can read out descriptions of their neighbours, giving examples of mutual help. (Be careful to weed out remarks likely to cause offence.)

Discuss how sometimes the only contact with neighbours seems to be through confrontation. Act out situations in which the children might be involved: trespassing to retrieve a ball; walking on garden walls; making excessive amounts of noise; or playing carelessly near the neighbours' car and damaging it. Two versions of the incident could be acted out; one which involves confrontation and the other where steps are taken to avoid it.

Talk about ways of encouraging positive relationships with neighbours, such as simple politeness, offering to help when the opportunity arises (the obvious examples are letter posting, shopping and gardening) and keeping a particularly careful watch on elderly neighbours, wherever possible.

Your own Coronation Street

Age range
Seven to twelve.

Presentation
Class.

What you need
Hymn 'Look out for Loneliness', *SSL*.
Prayer *LBCP* 87.

What to do
Set out a line of chairs, each facing the front. On each chair sits a child, dressed appropriately, representing the occupant of a house in your street. (If in doubt, use the Coronation Street characters as a starting point.) In turn, they tell a little about who they are and what they think about the other people in the street. Short scenes can then be acted out to show how these people may have differences but can pull together when necessary. For example, neighbours in the street may help someone to find a lost pet.

Use this assembly as a starting point for a Good Neighbour Scheme in your school's area. Local organisations and churches could be asked if there are ways in which older children could help, particularly with the care and visiting of the elderly and disabled.

Moving on

Age range
Five to nine.

Presentation
Teacher.

What you need
Hymn 'I've Just Moved into a New House', *TB*.
Story *Moving On*, Robert Lamb (see below).

What to do
Read the story *Moving On*. Use the story to draw out the children's own experiences of moving house and changing school – the feelings of sadness at leaving a place and people you know, the uncertainty about the new house and school.

At 11 o'clock the big blue removal van moved away from Jane's house. It filled the narrow lane and brushed down showers of autumn leaves. 'See you in Gloucester,' called the driver. Gloucester? She hardly knew where Gloucester was, but that was where she was going to live with mum and dad and their dog, Buz. Dad's firm had closed down the factory where he worked, but they had offered him a different job in Gloucester so, of course, he had to go. Jobs were hard to find where they lived.

'Hot drink, Jane?' called mum. 'Last one you'll ever get in number three.' What a thought! Inside the house, mum and dad were sitting on the stairs drinking their coffee. Jane sat on the bottom step sipping her drink. No one said much. They were each looking at the blank, curtainless windows, the bare floorboards and the light patches on the walls where the pictures had hung. What had once been a warm home was now a collection of cold empty boxes. All dad said was, 'Well, this is where this family began. I wonder how we'll end?' 'Come on, Jim,' said mum. 'It's people that make families, not houses, and you'll do well in your new job, if I know you. And I do.' Dad shook his head and looked gloomy so mum gave him a smacking kiss on his bald head. 'Into the car then,' sighed dad, 'and thanks for everything, number three.'

Jane had made up her mind not to cry. She knew that they were all sad and that crying would only make it worse, but her best friend came to say goodbye just as dad was about to turn the key in the door. In the flurry of packing she had forgotten Michelle, who was now holding out a brightly wrapped parcel. 'It's a goodbye present,' mumbled Michelle. That did it. Even mum started to blow her nose and Buz stopped wagging his tail for the first time ever. 'Oh, dear,' groaned dad.

Michelle stood in the lane and waved them out of sight. She looked very small and Jane knew she was really crying now because Michelle's shoulders always gave little hiccups when she cried. 'Don't forget to write!' called Jane out of the window, but they had already turned the bend and only a few brown cows looked up.

The countryside began to change, just like when you go on holiday – only they weren't going on holiday, they were leaving home. They were leaving Michelle and all her friends at school and they were leaving her teacher,

32

Miss Hughes, who made funny faces when she growled, 'You lot are 'orrible!' 'You're quiet in the back there,' said mum. 'Just sleepy,' said Jane. But really she was beginning to feel frightened about her new school in Gloucester. What would it be like? It was bound to be bigger. Gloucester was a city. The people were supposed to be rougher and tougher in the city. Would they be rough and tough with her?

As they joined the motorway it began to rain. Dad went on and on about everyone's crazy driving and Buz thought he was being told off so he stuck his head underneath Jane's coat. Miles and miles of nothing to see. She fell asleep and so did Buz.

When Jane woke up she heard dad say, 'At last, the Gloucester turn-off.' The countryside was a different

world now; a wide green plain with blue hills in the background. After a while, it became a jumble of red-brick houses and streets, traffic signs, shops and shoppers. 'Don't worry, Jane,' said mum, 'We don't live right in Gloucester. Where we live is nearly out into the countryside again.' 'I don't care where it is,' Jane thought, 'It isn't home.'

Their new house was like all the others in the street — small and a bit shabby — but dad said they were lucky to have a house at all. The blue van was there and the removal men were staggering into the house with the old green sofa that dad's sister had given them. 'You'd better keep out of the way for a while,' said dad. 'There's a shop just down there on the corner, so get yourself some

sweets.' He gave her 50p.

Jane bought her sweets from the scruffy newsagent's and was slowly walking back when two boys and a girl jumped out at her from behind a fence. Jane clutched her sweets to her chest.

'We don't want your sweets,' sneered the ginger haired girl.

'You the new people?' asked the blond boy.

'What's your name then?' said the boy on roller skates.

'Jane,' said the newcomer.

'Jane the pain, Jane the pain,' sang out the ginger girl.

'What school you going to then?' asked roller skates.

'Highfield,' remembered Jane.

'That's us. We go there,' they shouted.

'Do you like it?' asked Jane.

'Terrible. They keep you in and chuck chalk at you!' they all shouted with delight.

'It's not bad really,' said the ginger girl, wrinkling her nose. 'I bet your teacher'll be Mr Deane. He's like Rod Stewart.'

'We are sailing . . .', the boys started up but just then Buz ran barking down the street towards them. He was soon smothered in pats — which made Buz feel he could easily get to like Gloucester.

'Want a sweet?' said Jane holding out the bag. Three hands dived in.

'Want to see where the school is?' said the ginger girl. 'It's only across them fields.'

'Beat you there,' said roller skates. 'Me and Jerry against ginger nut and the bag of sweets.'

Suddenly Jane and Buz were chasing wildly down the street and across a wide playing field. Ginger nut grabbed her hand tightly. 'Come on!' she screamed, 'them boys think they're everything! We'll show 'em! Run, Jane, run!'

Robert Lamb

Living with other people

New things

Age range
Five to eleven.

Presentation
Teacher.

What you need
A range of stock new to the school – toys, bricks, books, pencils, crayons and even new furniture. Choose items that *look* particularly attractive and are preferably unopened.
Prayer *LPT*, page 8.

What to do
This assembly should be organised for the beginning of the school year. Talk about all the new things that the children will meet in the coming year – new teacher, new classroom, new work and new friends. Emphasise the excitement that we get from meeting new situations. Invite the children to talk about any new skills that they have learned during the holidays – maybe some of them have learned to swim or taken up a new hobby.

Show the children all the new things that you have found around the school. Point out how attractive they look and how the children can all help to keep them looking good.

What's your hobby?

Age range
Five to eleven.

Presentation
Teacher and enlisted helpers.

What you need
Information on school clubs, local youth clubs, junior clubs, Brownies, Cubs, majorettes, holiday time activities etc.

What to do
Try to find some colleagues willing to talk about their hobbies. Ask them to bring along some equipment that

they use, such as climbing gear, a musical instrument, a stamp album or a record collection.

Ask the children what a hobby is and if any of them have hobbies. Why do we have hobbies? Do adults have hobbies too? Then introduce the pre-selected staff who can talk about how their hobbies developed and how much time they spend on them. If possible, they can demonstrate their skills, particularly anyone with musical talents. Explain that hobbies are an expression of our own special interests and that through these activities we can meet friends who share our interests.

Children could be encouraged to share accounts of their own skills and talents, and to discuss why we have these and how we use them. This could be supported by a reading of Matthew 25, the parable of the talents. Using our talents fully helps make the world a better place.

Then describe some of the club facilities available locally and any clubs that you may have at school. Ask the children who attend the clubs to talk about what they do and why they joined. If possible, draw up a broadsheet with information and addresses of local clubs. A group of children could follow this up as a project, producing their own document.

Superpeople

Age range
Seven to twelve.

Presentation
Teacher and class.

What you need
Stories from *Superman*, *SuperGran* and *Super Ted*.
Music 'The Superman Theme'

What to do
In the classroom, discuss the nature of the super-characters with the children. What superpowers do they have? Do they use them for good or for evil? All the stories provide a simple dichotomy between the 'goodies' and the 'baddies'. Ask the children to imagine they have superpowers and what they might be able to do to work for good using their powers. The children can then paint pictures of themselves in a superstyle outfit and can write about *how* they would use their superpowers to help people. They might wish to dramatise their ideas. The Superpeople worksheet can also be used (see page 119).

Have the children introduce the assembly with a presentation of their pictures, writing and drama sequences. Discuss their superpowers and those of the more famous characters with the other children. Relate this to our knowledge of the unusual powers that Jesus possessed. What do we call the acts which he performed which would generally be considered impossible? Perhaps the children can tell you about some of his miracles, although this may need careful handling.

Brave people

Age range
Seven to twelve.

Presentation
Teacher.

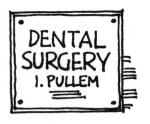

What you need
Collect information on brave deeds including well-known people such as Douglas Bader, Gandhi, Edith Cavell and Scott of the Antarctic. Find out about lesser known and preferably local personalities who are known for their bravery (newspaper reports often provide interesting local accounts).

What to do
Ask the children if they can think of any times when they had to be brave, such as going to the dentist, an accident, or the first time they stayed away from home. Tell the children about one or more of the brave deeds that you have researched. Try to emphasise the ordinary human qualities of the people concerned.

Grace Darling
Grace Darling lived on Longstone's Lighthouse in the Farne Islands. Her father was the lighthouse keeper. In 1838 the SS Forfarshire ran aground on the rocks during a storm. Grace and her father set out to rescue the crew in a small rowing boat. Fighting their way through heavy seas, they managed to rescue nine people. Both Grace and her father were awarded the Royal Humane Society's gold medal.

When I needed a neighbour

Age range
Seven to twelve.

Presentation
Teacher.

What you need
Story of The Good Samaritan (Luke, chapter 10 v25-37).
Hymn 'Cross over the Road', *CP*.
Prayer *LBFP* 80.

What to do
The Good Samaritan story could be given a modern setting. Racial tension in multi-ethnic communities could be used as the basis.

After pointing out the moral of the story, the wider context of the word 'neighbour' can be discussed. The children should be made aware that some regions of the world are torn apart by conflict; emphasise our need to support our neighbours in the Third World. The assembly could be part of a fund-raising effort, or a class project to learn more about a particular area. Personal links could be made through local churches or national societies and charities. Point out that, to be good neighbours at whatever level, we need a spirit of friendship, which may be one-sided at first but is likely to develop into a two-way process.

This assembly could be linked with other assemblies on similar themes, such as Compassion (see page 42).

Turning the other cheek

Age range
Eight to twelve.

Presentation
Teacher.

What you need
Martin Luther King's famous speech, 'I Have a Dream'.
Prayer: *LBCP* 14, 37 (prayer of St Francis); *WYP* 203.
Songs 'Getting Angry', *ECS*; 'Down by the Riverside', *NO*.

Martin Luther King.

What to do
When Jesus told his followers to 'turn the other cheek', he wasn't instructing them to be cowardly and walk away from difficult situations, but rather to face up to them without the use of violence (Matthew 5).

This was the teaching that Martin Luther King followed. Tell the children about the life and work of Martin Luther King. He was born and grew up in Georgia, America. Everywhere in Georgia in those days there were signs saying 'No coloureds' and 'Whites only'. King, who had a black skin, knew that this was wrong.

In 1955 he started a peaceful protest to make a bus company change its rules so that black people could sit anywhere on its buses and not have to give up their places to white people.

He led many protests, but always peaceful ones, and in 1964 he was awarded the Nobel Peace Prize. In 1968, whilst he was trying to help some poorly paid workers to protest about their wages, he was killed by a gunman.

Read the extract from 'I Have a Dream'. Relate the work of Martin Luther King to the current peaceful campaign led by Bishop Tutu in South Africa. The children could follow up this assembly by finding out more about the Nobel Peace Prize and research some of the recent winners.

Sharing

Age range
Five to eight.

Presentation
Teacher and small group of children.

What you need
Some sweets, a pot of crayons and some paper,
Plasticine, a storybook, a box of Lego and a hand-
puppet.
Story *One Eighth of a Muffin*, Ruth Orbach, Jonathan
Cape, 1984.

What to do
Select two children. Ask them to share an even number
and then an odd number of sweets. Involve all the
children in discussing the fairness of what the children
do. Then do the same with the other materials, paying
particular attention to how they share the puppet as this
will involve taking turns. Broaden the discussion to
include things that we have to share at home and at
school.

Now tell the story *One Eighth of a Muffin* in shortened
form. The story is about two girls who are always
squabbling over things that they have to share. Their
parents seek the help of a wise old man who tells them to
ask each girl to invite a friend to stay. The story follows
this pattern until there are 16 children and two adults in
the tiny house. The wise man than tells them to send their
friends home and the girls find that they are now able to
share.

The story has more impact if it is dramatised. Children
can be selected to take part as the story progresses. A PE
mat can be used to represent the space of the tiny house.

Compassion

Age range
Seven to eleven.

Presentation
Teacher and class.

What you need
Information on Bob Geldof and Band Aid. Fundraising posters/pictures about Ethiopia and other Third World countries.
Hymn 'God, Whose Name is Love', *LBHS*.
Prayer *TAP*, page 50.
Music 'Do They Know It's Christmas?'.

What to do
With the class prepare two improvisations, one showing a person who feels sorry for and tries to help another person, the other showing the exact opposite. Start the assembly with the two scenes and the children are asked to discuss the value of compassion and recall times when they felt sorry for other people.

Play part of 'Do They Know It's Christmas?'. Children in the class can present information about Bob Geldof and Band Aid or another topical charity – perhaps in the form of a TV report.

Use this assembly as a starting point for raising money for Ethiopia and Sudan (or another region that is topical).

Information on the latest projects can be obtained from Band Aid, PO Box 4TX, London W1A 4TX.

This assembly could be linked with other assemblies on a similar theme, such as Water is life (see page 54), You are what you eat (see page 65), or When I needed a neighbour (see page 39).

Mind your manners

Age range
Seven to twelve.

Presentation
Teacher and class.

What you need
A useful starting point is *Perfect Pigs; An Introduction to Manners*, Marc Brown & Stephen Krensky, Collins.

What to do
Before the assembly the class can think of some familiar social rules that they have heard such as 'Don't eat with your mouth full', 'Say please', 'Knock before you enter' and so on. The *Perfect Pigs* book provides an excellent humorous introduction to what could be a rather starchy topic. The children could make up contrasting drama sequences to demonstrate the presence, or lack of, good manners.

Begin the assembly by discussing what is meant by 'Mind your manners'. Why should people have good manners? Talk about the effect that our behaviour has on others and how we can try not to offend or upset other people. The children can present their drama sequences to highlight the points made.

For younger children the story of *The Elephant and the Bad Baby* by Elfrida Vipont and Raymond Briggs (Picture Puffins) emphasises the point.

Co-operation

Age range
Five to twelve.

Presentation
Teacher.

What you need
The Co-operative Sports and Games Book: challenge without competition, Terry Orlick, Writers & Readers Publishing Co-operative Ltd.

What to do
Ask the children to think of any work, jobs or games that they have done recently which involved the co-operation of other people, for example lifting a heavy object, tidying away the toys or playing in a sports team with other people. Would they have been able to achieve as much if they had worked alone? Can anyone explain what co-operation means?

Explain that you are going to teach the children some games in which no one is out and the fun of the game depends on everyone working together to help each other. Select a group of children to try some of the following games.

1 Non-elimination musical chairs
The game is played in the same way as traditional musical chairs but each time a chair is removed all the children have to share the chairs that are left! Each time a chair is removed the children have to sit on parts of chairs or each other, in order to keep everyone in the game. The game ends with all the children attempting to perch on one chair.

2 The more we get together
A group of four children form a circle and dance round whilst singing:
The more we get together,
Together, together.
The more we get together,
The happier we'll be.
For your friends are my friends,
And my friends are your friends.
The more we get together,
The happier we'll be.

At the end of each chorus they each go and choose a new friend to join in.

3 Can you do things together?

The object of this game is for the children to perform a task or act out a motion with one or more friends. Here are some suggestions – no doubt you and the children can think up many more.

Can you be one frog with your partner?

Can you make a human chair for your partner to sit on? A two-people chair? A four-people chair?

With your back stuck to your partner's back, can you move around the room? Jump forwards towards the wall? Both get inside a hoop and move around, still back to back?

4 Non-verbal birthday line up

A group of children are asked to line up according to the month and day of birth 'without any talking'. This should inspire some interesting means of communication towards a common goal.

Ask the children to note the times in the next week when it will be necessary for them to co-operate with others in some activity. Can they think of ways of improving co-operation within their class?

Responsibility and caring

Age range
Five to twelve.

Presentation
Teacher.

What you need
A school pet (rabbit, gerbil etc) or, if your school does not have pets, arrange for one of the children to bring in a suitable pet.
Prayers *LBCP* 16/17; *LPT* 11; *WYP* 192.
Songs 'All Creatures of our God and King', *NO/CP*;
'When God made the Garden of Creation', *CP*.

What to do
Tell the children about the pet. How long has the school owned it? What does it eat? How often is it fed? What is in its cage? Who organises the food and the cleaning of the cage? Who looks after it in the school holidays? Ask for examples of other sorts of pet kept at home. Get the child owners to describe what's involved in looking after them – bring out the cons as well as the pros, if you can. For example, dogs need walking even in bad weather; the smelly cages of rabbits and guinea pigs need cleaning out; horses need mucking out and grooming. Remember that many children long for a pet and haven't got one. But those who have may admit that their mothers and fathers have to do the 'looking after' once the novelty wears off.

Joe Homan's Boys' Town

Age range
Seven to twelve.

Presentation
Teacher.

What you need
Further information available from: International Boys' Town Trust, 50 Willesden Avenue, Walton, Peterborough.

What to do
Tell the children how Joe Homan came to set up the Boys' Towns. In 1965 Joe Homan gave up teaching in England and returned to southern India, where he had been saddened by the sight of ragged children begging and dying on the pavements that were their homes.

He took £200 of his own money, borrowed a piece of land and invited homeless lads to help him build a poultry farm. Together they made mud bricks and built a thatched house and five poultry sheds. In six months they had a flourishing farm with a thousand hens.

More boys drifted in and, with help from English schools and a grant from Oxfam, Joe bought 22 acres of semi-desert land – his first Boys' Town.

Soon there were 80 children at Tirumangalem; today Joe runs seven Boys' Towns in southern India and a girls' home is being developed into a fully fledged Girls' Town. Altogether more than 700 children are cared for.

It is possible to sponsor a child from the Boys' Town – the sum of £60 will keep a boy or girl for one year. More information is available from the above address. Joe is sometimes able to visit schools on his occasional trips back to England.

The environment

The cycle of life

Age range
Five to nine.

Presentation
Teacher.

What you need
A quantity of leaf mould in various forms of decay. A wormery. Reproduce the diagram of the cycle of change.

Hymns 'Autumn Days', *CP*; 'Autumn', *ECS*.
Prayers *LBCP*, page 74; *LBFP*, page 53.

What to do
Death is an important part of the cycle of life and needs to be brought to children's notice in a sensitive and reassuring manner. One such way is to make use of the leaves that fall in the autumn — extra quantities available from your local parks and gardens department. Deposited in heaps, they naturally turn into high-grade leaf mould. Aided by worms, the leaves are mixed into the earth, and existing plants, new plants and worms thrive in the fertilised soil. It takes time for these changes to occur, and one way of demonstrating the rate of change and how it takes place is to have a wormery in school and to see the leaves slowly disappear over a period of weeks.

Introduce the worms to the wormery during the assembly. Explain the process, using the diagram. This should help the children to focus on the idea of the continuity of life, and the fact that we are all interdependent. Mount leaves in various stages of decay onto card to illustrate the process. Encourage the children to handle the leaf mould so that they can appreciate its value in our environment.

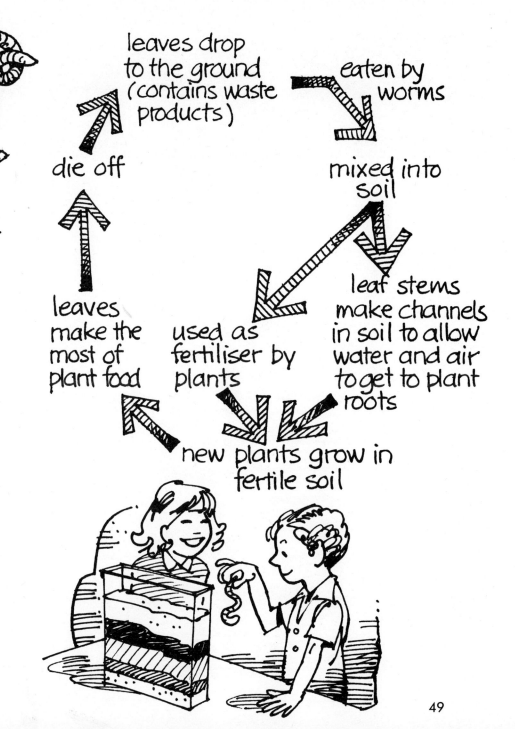

leaves drop to the ground (contains waste products)

eaten by worms

die off

mixed into soil

leaf stems make channels in soil to allow water and air to get to plant roots

leaves make the most of plant food

used as fertiliser by plants

new plants grow in fertile soil

Homes

Age range
Five to twelve.

Presentation
Teacher.

What you need
Pictures of homes from around the world.
Prayer *LBCP* 10/11.
Song 'A House is a House for Me', *TB*; 'We're Going Home', *SSL*.

What to do
Ask two or three children to describe their homes. What do they particularly like about their homes? Where do they feel most comfortable and safe? Encourage the children to think of some words to complete 'A home is a place where . . .'

Show the children the pictures of homes from other countries. Talk about why the houses are different — building materials, the physical terrain, the climate etc. Have any of the children ever moved house? How did they feel when they left their old homes? Imagine what it would be like if you had to leave your home but had nowhere else to go. Explain that all over the world there are families who are homeless and others who had to leave their homes because of war or famine. Tell the children about the charity, Shelter.

my house

Feeding the birds

Age range
Five to eleven.

Presentation
Teacher and small group of children.

What you need
Scraps of food suitable for wild birds, eg strings of peanuts, suet pudding, half a coconut; some pictures of birds seen in the winter.
Music 'Feed the Birds' *Mary Poppins*.

What to do
Being aware of the needs of those around us, humans or animals, is an important part of living life to the full. In winter, birds are particularly vulnerable and need help.

It is best to organise this assembly during the cold winter months when the birds are most in need of food. Arrange for a small group of children to bring in some scraps of food suitable for birds.

Start by showing the children the pictures of the birds and find out how many they can identify. Ask the children to tell you about the birds that visit their gardens or balconies. Do all the birds stay here for the winter? What happens to the others? Ask them to think where the birds get food from in the winter. Have any of them found holes in their milk bottle tops?

Arrange for a group of children to bring in some scraps of food that would be suitable for wild birds. They can talk about what they have brought and discuss where would be a good place to put it out. This may inspire some children to build a bird table.

Busy bees

Age range
Five to twelve.

Presentation
Teacher.

What you need
A jar of honey; pictures of bees; if possible, some borrowed bee-keeping equipment, eg a smoke, a piece of honeycomb, a bee-keeper's veil.
Books *Honeybees*, J B Free, A & C Black; *The Life Cycle of the Honeybee*, P Hogan, Ward Lock Educational.
Music 'The Flight Of The Bumblebee' by Rimsky-Korsakov.
Prayers *TWI*, pages 14, 61, 65
Song 'The Beehive', *SAS*.

What to do
Show the children the jar of honey, and ask them if they know where the honey comes from. Explain that honey-bees, not bumble-bees, produce honey. Tell the children about the organisation of the honey-bee colony (see next column). Emphasise that each bee has its own special job to do – laying eggs, cleaning the hive, finding food and so on. All these jobs are equally important for the survival of the colony. Compare this with human organisations such as a family or school, where the smooth running of the place and the happiness of all involved depends on everyone contributing something.

A bee-keeper must respect the organisation of the colony and needs to understand how the bees live in order to look after them properly. Show the children the bee-keeping equipment. The bee-keeper needs to handle the bees carefully and gently so that they do not become perturbed.

The organisation of a bee colony
The queen bee is the mother of all the other bees in the colony. She lays the eggs, sometimes as many as several hundred each day. Most of the bees in the colony are workers. These are the female bees. They do all kinds of jobs, including finding and collecting food, feeding the queen and the larvae, cleaning the hive, building and repairing the honeycomb, and fighting off intruders.

Some of the cells in the hive are for food, others are for eggs. After three days, the eggs grow into larvae. These are fed by the nurse bees. After five days, the larvae become pupae, and the worker bees cap the cell with wax. Thirty days later, the pupae develop into fully grown worker bees which bite their way through the wax caps. Queen bees are reared in special cells called queen cups, and are given special food called royal jelly.

Bees are able to signal information to each other by performing specific 'dance' movements. For example, when a worker finds a food supply, she will perform a special dance in the form of a figure eight. This tells the other bees in which direction and how far away the food can be found.

Down on the farm

Age range
Five to eight.

Presentation
Teacher and class.

What you need
Song 'Old MacDonald had a Farm'.
The children can make animal puppets
using paper plates and junk
modelling materials. These are
used with the song.
Story *The Little Red Hen*, a traditional
tale, Ladybird.
Hymn 'The Farmer Comes to Scatter the Seed', *SSL*.
Prayer *LPT*, page 14.

What to do
With the class prepare a drama sequence telling the story
of the little red hen. This could be acted out by the
children or by using puppets.

Tell the children about the jobs that the farm workers
are likely to be doing at this time of year. Explain that
both the animals and the land need to be looked after
well if they are to keep healthy. Emphasise the long hours
and the range of jobs that farm workers have to do.
Make up a short farm quiz to find out what the children
know about farming.

During the assembly the class can sing 'Old
MacDonald had a farm', holding up the appropriate
puppets for each verse.

Let them act out the story of *The Little Red Hen*. This
story highlights the work and patience involved in
growing crops and the importance of working together.

Water is life

Age range
Five to eleven.

Presentation
Teacher only or teacher and class.

What you need
Charity and other posters depicting drought, irrigation and the need for water; other pictures of water, rain, storms, rivers, waterfalls and leisure activities connected with water.
Hymn 'Water of Life', *CP*.
Prayer *TAP*, no 52.
Story *Tiddalick: The Frog Who Caused a Flood*. An Adaption of an Aboriginal Dreamtime Legend, Picture Puffin.

What to do
Pour out a glass of water and open a can of coke. Ask a child to select which he or she would prefer and then ask them which is more important to us. Explain that we need water to make coke and lots of other things that we eat and drink. Get the children to think of some other uses for water – washing clothes, sewage, transport, making electricity and so on.

Then show the children the charity poster depicting the effects of drought and talk about the needs of people living in areas of drought. Ask the children how we can help them, both through monetary aid and more direct action – Oxfam projects, appropriate technology etc.

Read *Tiddalick*. When Tiddalick drinks all the rivers in the land the effect on the other animals is devastating. The story tells how they manage to get the water back.

Before or after the assembly, children could prepare work on the following themes: Water is food; Water is health; Water is transport; Water is fun; Water is life.

This assembly could be linked with other assemblies on similar themes such as You are what you eat (see page 65) and Health for all (see page 69).

Dinosaurs and all that rubbish

Age range
Five to eleven.

Presentation
Teacher.

What you need
A selection of rubbish – crisp packets, broken bottles, opened cans etc; a bin liner containing a selection of rubbish which provides clues about the owner; some models and artwork produced by children using various forms of junk.
Story *Dinosaurs and All That Rubbish*, Michael Foreman, Picture Puffin.

What to do
Show the children the collection of rubbish and talk about the constituents – plastic, card, glass, decaying matter etc. Ask them if they can tell you the difference between litter and rubbish. Where should we put litter? Discuss the possible dangers of litter – accidents, spread of germs, pollution of the countryside, harm to animals and so on.

Produce the bin liner and explain that you are going to show the children the contents and ask them to use these as clues to help them to work out what sort of person used the contents. For example, empty tins of baby food indicate that there is a baby in the family.

Read *Dinosaurs and All That Rubbish*. 'One day, when Man had set out for a distant star, the dinosaurs came back to life and tidied up the barren wastes he had left behind him. Man was only allowed back when he agreed that the Earth should be shared and enjoyed by everyone.'

To conclude the assembly, explain that rubbish can also be used positively and creatively. Show the children's art and craft work pointing out what junk was used. Also mention the use of bottle banks and the recycling of paper.

Animals in danger

Age range
Seven to twelve.

Presentation
Teacher.

Green Turtle

Giant Panda

What you need
The following series of books provides useful background information: *Animals in Danger*, Chambers. There are five titles, covering disappearing animals in North America, The Forests of Africa, The Seas, Europe and Asia.

Useful organisations include the following: The Flora and Fauna Preservation Society, c/o Zoological Society of London, Regent's Park, London; The Otter Trust, Earsham, Near Bungay, Suffolk; The Royal Society for the Protection of Birds, The Lodge, Sandy, Bedfordshire; Wildlife Youth Service, Marston Court, 98–106 Manor Road, Wallington, Surrey; World Wildlife Fund, 11–13 Ockford Road, Godalming, Surrey.

Blue Whale

North Atlantic Right Whale

What to do
Ask the children if they have heard the expression 'as dead as a dodo'. Do they know what it means? What was a dodo? Explain that many animals have become extinct – some, like dinosaurs, because of climatic changes, but some because of the activities of people. Ask for examples of how people can make life difficult for animals.

Most of the children will have heard of the Save the Whale campaign. At present, there are 14 types of whale whose survival is in danger. The hunting of whales for their meat and other products has been the main threat.

Oil from whales is used to soften leather and to make soap, crayons, lipstick and perfumes. Fertilisers, glue and pet food are also made from whale products. All these products can be made by other means, often without killing animals at all. At present, many countries are trying to achieve a total ban on whaling, at least until the whales are able to raise their numbers again. If this does not happen, we may well lose some species of these fascinating creatures for ever.

Otters are also at risk. In some countries, they are still hunted for sport, even though their skins are of little value. They are regarded as a nuisance by some people because they can damage fish hatcheries; however, these could easily be protected from otters. The main threat to otters comes from pollution. Many of our rivers have been polluted by sewage, chemicals and waste from factories. These pollutants affect not only otters, but also all life in rivers. The increased number of power boats, cruisers and picnickers has forced otters to retreat to more remote sites, and these sites are now limited in number.

Encourage the children to find out more about animals in danger, through the organisations listed.

Otter

Gorilla

Signs around us

Age range
Seven to twelve.

Presentation
Teacher and class.

What you need
Pictures of road signs, shop signs and old trade signs; washing labels on clothing, warnings on electrical appliances, health and safety signs (available from the Health Education Council, 78 New Oxford St, London WC1).
Prayer Thomas a Kempis (1380–1471): 'Grant us, Lord, to know that which is worth knowing and to love that which is worth loving. Grant us, with true judgement, to distinguish things that are different and, above all, to reach out and do what is right. Amen.'
Song 'One More Step', CP 17.

What to do
Ask the children in your class to collect examples of signs that they see at home, in school, in their locality. The children could invent signs for use in school, such as 'No running', 'Quiet please'. Make drawings and paintings of the signs and discuss what they mean; are they orders, do they give warnings or do they just provide information?
Start the assembly by using hand signals telling the children to stand up, sit down, come to you, fetch a book etc. Talk about how we use our hands for signalling and how deaf people rely on sign language. The children can then present their signs and talk about their functions. They could do this in the form of a quiz to find out how many of the signs the other children understand.

Make a distinction between the different things signs say: a chemist's coloured jars or a pub sign may simply say, 'Look, I'm here!'; some road signs say, 'Take care!'; other road signs give us orders – 'Do this' or 'Don't do that'. Often, signs make us think and decide how we should act. This assembly could be linked to those on Road safety (see page 61) and Warnings (see page 62).

'I Spy' on my way to school

Age range
Five to twelve.

Presentation
Teacher and children.

What you need
Photocopies of the worksheet on page 120.
Prayers *LPT*, pages 4–7; *BCP*, page 12.
Songs 'All the Things Which Live Below the Sky', *SSL*; 'I Love God's Tiny Creatures', *SSL*; 'Morning has Broken', *CP*; 'He Gave Me Eyes So I Could See', *SSL*; 'Give to us Eyes', *SSL*; 'Praise to God for Things We See', *SSL*.

What to do
This assembly aims to make children more aware of their local environment. Encourage the children to look carefully for interesting things on their way to school. They should not only notice things that happen to catch their attention, but also actively look around them, under stones, above their heads and in trees. They should also listen carefully. Explain that small finds are just as significant as larger, more dramatic ones. The emphasis of the exercise is on becoming good 'scientists' and being able to provide a clear, detailed description of observations. Use the 'I Spy' photocopiable worksheet to record children's findings.

In the assembly the children could simply describe their observations or present written accounts and illustrations. This could develop into a series of assemblies with classes taking it in turns to present their observations. You may like to set up an 'I Spy' display area in school or duplicate 'I Spy' recording sheets (see illustration). Observations made at different times of the year could be used to heighten children's awareness of the changing seasons.

Supplement the children's observations with stories and poems about some of the things that they have found.

Health and safety

Road safety

Age range
Five to twelve.

Presentation
Teacher, a small group of children, possibly a road safety officer.

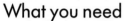

What you need
A poster depicting the Green Cross Code; luminous clothing, arm bands, reflectors etc; The sequence for traffic lights and crossing patrol indicators, reproduced on card; a tape-recording of a busy road including horns beeping, screeching of brakes and the bleeping of a pedestrian crossing.

What to do
Play the tape-recording of road noises. Ask the children to tell you what is happening. Explain that lots of accidents occur on roads – why do the children think that is? Which roads near your school are particularly dangerous, and why?

Ask for volunteers to demonstrate the Green Cross Code. Some children on bikes could be involved to represent the traffic. Talk about the safe places to cross roads and the need to watch the lights on a pedestrian crossing. Explain that it is important to set an example to younger children who might not understand the rules of the road. A link could be made to the assemblies on Signs around us (see page 58) and Warnings (see page 62).

How many children have a bike? Have any of them taken the road cycling proficiency test and, if so, can they come and talk about what they had to learn? Show the children the luminous clothing etc and talk about when it needs to be worn. Ask if any of the children can sort out the sequence of the traffic lights. Further information is available from RoSPA, Cannon House, The Priory Queensway, Birmingham B4 6BS.

Warnings

Age range
Five to twelve.

Presentation
Teacher (and class).

What you need
Warning signs printed clearly on card.
Song 'If I Had a Hammer', *SSL*.

What to do
Start off by asking the children what it means if someone says 'I'm warning you!'. A warning is a message which tells you to watch out.

Show the children the various warning signs/symbols. Can they read/interpret them? Where and when would they see them? Can they think of any more? Do they notice anything special about the signs – colour, size, clarity and so on. Explain that warnings need to be as simple and as clear as possible.

Can the children think of any dangerous places around the school or the neighbourhood. Are there any warning signs? If not, perhaps some of the children could invent their own. Following the assembly, the children could do a survey of the playground to find out where and how frequently accidents occur. They could then make recommendations for improving the safety of the playground.

This assembly could be linked to those on Signs around us (see page 58) and Road safety (see page 61).

Firework safety

Age range
Five to eleven.

Presentation
Teacher.

What you need
Posters on firework safety and the Firework Code; a display of fireworks, sparklers, a pair of gloves, a wick and some matches; a guy made by some of the children; a flipboard and pen.

What to do
Arrange for some of the children to bring on the guy, calling 'penny for the guy'. Ask the children if they know why it is called a guy and why we celebrate Bonfire Night.

Show the children the fireworks and talk about the fun and excitement of watching them go off. Find out if any of the children are going to any big firework displays. Discuss other occasions when fireworks are used, such as Chinese New Year, Diwali or Royal celebrations.

Having emphasised the enjoyment to be had on Bonfire Night, then point out that all this can be ruined if any accidents occur because someone has not used fireworks safely. Get the children to tell you why fireworks can be dangerous and what they can do to prevent accidents happening. With their aid write out a school firework code on a flipboard. Compare this with the published Firework Code.

You may be able to arrange for a safety officer from your local council to come and talk to them about the dangers.

Following the assembly, groups of children could reproduce the Firework Code in poster form.

Recipe for life

Age range
Eight to twelve.

Presentation
Teacher and class.

What to do
Look at various recipes and other forms of instructions with the children. Distinguish between the ingredients and processes. Extend this idea to producing a recipe for health, including ingredients such as avoidance of stress, the inadvisability of smoking and the need for regular exercise. Other possibilities are: A recipe for failure; A recipe for friendship; A recipe for peace; A recipe for disaster; A recipe for happiness.

    Groups of children could present ideas connected with their particular recipe in the form of a cookery demonstration.

You are what you eat

Age range
Eight to twelve.

Presentation
Teacher.

What you need
The poems 'You are what you eat' and 'Famine' by Bob Docherty.
Hymn 'The Body Song', *SLW*.
Prayer *HMP* 60.

What to do
First of all, read the poem 'You are what you eat'. You could illustrate this by bringing in some food to represent the average daily intake in the Western world. Can the children tell you how food makes you what you are? What do we mean by a balanced diet, and what happens if we have too much or too little food? Now read the poem 'Famine'. Explain what can happen to people when they suffer from malnutrition. Have the children any ideas on how we can share our resources better? Perhaps they have already been involved in some fund raising effort.

This assembly could be linked with other assemblies on a similar theme, such as Water is life (see page 54) and Health for all (see page 69).

Famine

Some live in comfort,
Enjoying their wealth.
They eat far too much
And suffer ill health.

Ethiopian children
At night go to bed
Having eaten too little,
No fruit and no bread.

But there *is* enough food
In spite of the drought,
Disease, greed and war –
If we shared it all out.

And the starving child asks:
'Then can you explain,
Why I live through each day
On a handful of grain?'

You Are What You Eat

My mum said to me
While having our tea
That we are what we eat – and it's true!
For it's clear that my legs
Are composed of fried eggs
And my feet made of vegetable stew.

You can see that my eyes
Are both made of mince pies.
My neck's made of scones, buns and cakes.
My ears and my cheeks
Are carrots and leeks
And my chin's made of soggy cornflakes.

This tummy protruding
Is mostly rice pudding.
My arms are stewed apples and custard.
I think that my hair's
Made of chocolate éclairs
And my nose of sausage and mustard.

I'd say that my lips
Are fish fingers and chips
So whatever is left must be made
Of what I like most –
Hot, buttered toast
And lashings of Mum's marmalade.

The opening door

Age range
Seven to twelve.

Presentation
Teacher.

What you need
The Opening Door, by John Stephens available from Adult Education Central Area, Gladstone House, 28 St Giles Street, Norwich; *Joey: An unforgettable story of human courage*, Joseph Deacon, Charles Scribner's Sons; *I use a wheelchair*, Althea, Dinosaur.

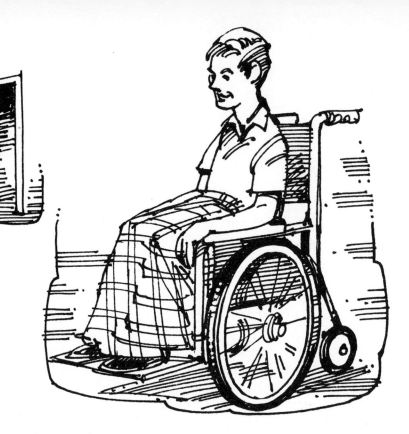

What to do
Explain to the children that many people are born with or develop physical disabilities. The extent to which they are handicapped by these disabilities depends on many things such as devices to help their mobility or improve their sight or hearing, access to facilities such as ramps and lifts, and also their own and other people's willingness to help them overcome their disabilities. For younger children the book *I use a wheelchair* provides a clear insight into the feelings and frustrations experienced by a young disabled person.

Explain that you are going to tell the children about two people who through extraordinary effort were able to overcome considerable physical difficulties in order to write a record of their own personal experiences.

John

John Stephens was born in Bishop's Stortford in the 1930s. He spent his childhood in London and moved to Lowestoft in 1953. John is spastic and did not go to any school. He had various tutors at home and gradually learned to read. With great difficulty he types, using a special lever positioned over the keyboard of a typewriter.

Some years ago John became a resident at Bishop Herbert House in Norwich. There he received help from the Adult Literacy Service. The following is an extract from his book *The Opening Door*.

'I lived with Mum until I came to live at Bishop Herbert House. After being here for a while, I realised that there *was* a lot to live for. I was encouraged to do things for myself without being forced. I had never drunk a cup of tea by myself. One of the care assistants said to me one day, "I bet you can drink that by yourself."

I said "I bet I can't. I would upset it." She said: "That doesn't matter. I will make sure it doesn't go over you." She put the mug of tea with my plastic straw on the table and stayed with me while I had a go.

It was a marvellous feeling to do something so simple that I had never done before.'
John

Joey

Joey Deacon lived in a hospital for the mentally and physically handicapped for most of his life. Joey decided to write his life story but was only able to do this with the help of three fellow residents. Joey has cerebral palsy which seriously affects all four limbs and speech. His friend Ernie is the only person who can really understand him; he cannot read and write. So Ernie listened to Joey's story and then repeated it to Michael who wrote it down. The hand-written version was then typed by Tom who worked at the rate of four to six lines per day. Through this incredible team effort they were able to produce a weighty volume, a very moving story about a man whose extraordinary self-discipline and courage allowed him to look beyond himself; to expect no special recompense and to stand as much as possible on his own.

First aid

Age range
Seven to twelve.

Presentation
Teacher.

What you need
Information available from the Red Cross, 14 Grosvenor Crescent, London SW1. *The First Aid Handbook.*
Prayers *LBCP*, page 41; *TAP* no 46; *LPT*, page 34.
Songs 'For All the Strength We Have', *SSL*; 'People Who Help Us', *NCF*; 'Love is Something if You Give it Away', *ST*.

What to do
Florence Nightingale and Mary Seacole were pioneers in the development of first aid and the improvement in hygiene and conditions in hospitals. Tell the children about their lives and work.

Explain that the Red Cross continues to take medical help to troubled areas of the world where there are wars, famine and refugees on the move.

Find out if any of the children have any knowledge of first aid through involvement in the Red Cross or Scout and Guide movements. They may like to demonstrate their skills.

Florence Nightingale
Florence, who was born in 1820, grew up in northern England. She came from a rich family and had a good education. When she was 25 she decided to train as a nurse, a profession of which her parents did not approve – they felt it did not befit a well bred young lady. Despite their opposition Florence went to Germany to train as a nurse.

In 1854 she took 38 nurses to the Crimea where she established hospital units at Scutari and Balaklava for victims of the war. At that time conditions in hospitals were appalling – dirty, overcrowded, no hot water, very little bedding and no medicine. Florence imposed high standards of hygiene and care and was able to reduce the death rate amongst army casualties from 42 per cent to 2 per cent in just over six months. The soldiers called her 'The Lady with the Lamp' because she carried an oil-lamp during her night visits.

On her return to England after the war Florence founded the nurses' training institution, at St Thomas's Hospital in London, which is still used to train nurses today.

Mary Seacole
As a young girl in Jamaica, Mary Seacole often helped her mother in her work looking after people who were ill. When there was an epidemic of a terrible disease, such as cholera, Mary was very busy, helping the sick. She learned a lot about nursing and medicines.

Some years later, she heard about the war being fought in the Crimea and set off to help the wounded soldiers there. First she went to London, where she was told she could not go because she was coloured – but she still went! When she got there, she was not allowed to open a hospital because of her black skin. Instead, she opened what was called a hotel. Soon it was full of wounded soldiers and Mary was working hard to make them better; just as another woman, more famous in England, was doing nearby – Florence Nightingale.

Health for all

Age range
Five to twelve.

Presentation
Teacher.

What you need
Some soap, a toothbrush, a jug of clean water, fresh vegetables, a first aid tin, a bicycle and a nurse's outfit. Prayer *LBCP* 22.

What to do
Show the children the selected items and ask them what these have to do with keeping healthy. Talk about the need for good food, clean water, simple health and hygiene care. The bicycle represents the need to keep fit; the first aid tin and nurse's outfit stand for basic medical care.

Ask the children what it might be like in a country where you couldn't get clean water from a tap, or there was a shortage of water for washing and cleaning and a limited food supply. Talk about the spread of disease. Tell the children something about the work of the Save the Children Fund (address see page 124) with its emphasis on self-help and primary health care. The latter involves training village health workers and traditional birth attendants, running immunisation campaigns against childhood diseases, improving water supplies and basic sanitation and helping communities to grow better crops.

Ask the children about their own experiences at the local clinic. Do they know which diseases they have been immunised against?

This assembly could be linked with other assemblies on similar themes, such as Water is life (see page 54).

Interesting events

TV-am

Age range
Eight to eleven.

Presentation
Class.

What you need
Any props that the children require for their show, such as a weather map, presenter's chair, clipboard and news-script.

What to do
This assembly focuses attention on local community life, with an interesting format.

One class prepares its own version of *TV-am*, with news items including both good and bad news of local interest. Try to include all aspects of the community – jumble sales, clubs, lost pets, help required, births etc. If possible, include an interview with a local dignitary such as the vicar or the school cook, or discuss the hazards of crossing the road with the crossing patrol person. Other items could include a cookery spot, book reviews, viewers' comments and the inevitable weather forecast.

The presence of a few technicians, a clipboard, lighting effects and real 'live' hitches will add to the drama. You might even be able to borrow a video camera and record the event!

Space exploration

Age range
Seven to twelve.

Presentation
Teacher.

What you need
Stories and poems *Meg on the Moon*, Jan Pienkowski and Helen Nicholl, Picture Puffin; *Moon Man*, Ungerer, Methuen; *Legends of the Sun and Moon* E & T Hadley, Cambridge University Press; *Katy and the Nurgla*, Sir Harry Secombe, Young Puffin; *Spaceman, Spaceman and other Rhymes*, Barbara Ireson, Carousel.

What to do
Make a list of interesting events in the history of space exploration. You might include October 4, 1957 – Russia launched the first Sputnik; April 12, 1961 – Yuri Gagarin became the first man into space; May 15, 1961 – Alan Shephard became the first American astronaut; July 1969 – Neil Armstrong became the first man to set foot on the moon.

Talk about the excitement and wonder that goes with each stage in the history of space exploration. Why do the children think that people want to explore space? Do they find space interesting themselves? Discuss the pleasure gained from finding out about the unknown and historical interest in the mysteries of space. As well as talking about the thrill and glamour connected with space travel, some mention should be made of the dangers and the tragic events that have occurred, such as the Space Shuttle disaster of 1986. You could also mention and discuss the well-documented 'religious' experiences of astronauts.

Select a suitable story or poem about space. The selection of poems in *Spaceman, Spaceman and other Rhymes* provides a humorous insight into the world of space-flight.

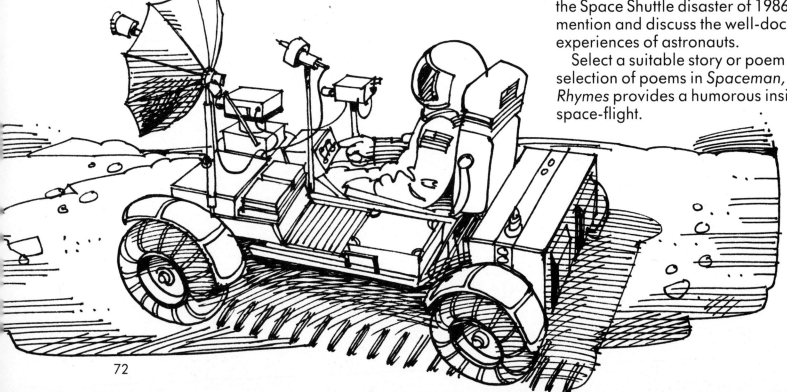

The mayor's visit

Age range
Five to twelve.

Presentation
Teacher with the help of the mayor.

What you need
Newspaper cuttings about recent functions attended by the mayor.

What to do
Many schools are near towns where they have a mayor. Children could discuss what a mayor is, why we have one, and how you can become one. If possible arrange for your mayor to visit your school dressed in full regalia. Ask the children to prepare questions about his/her office and duties. What does she/he like doing most and least? With younger children, you could show extracts from a television programme illustrating some of the jobs the mayor had to do.

In your introduction refer to newspaper cuttings describing the range of functions and events that the mayor has attended. Try to get your mayor to talk about his/her personal interests, family, job etc, as well as official duties. This could lead on to a project to find out more about the history and traditions of your area.

The school outing

Age range
Five to twelve.

Presentation
Teacher and group of children who have been on an outing.

What you need
A large map to show where they went; any interesting finds from the trip.
Prayer *LBCP*, page 27.
Songs 'The Train is A-coming', *AP*; 'The Wheels on the Bus', *OK*.

What to do
The atmosphere on a school outing is quite different from any other school day. Try to capture this in the assembly, particularly the excitement, the shared experience and the involvement of extra helpers – parents, dinner ladies etc (sneaky tape-recordings could help here). Arrange for the children to describe where they went, how they got there, any pre-planning that they had to do, and for them to give a selection of personal comments on the day.

The marathon

Age range
Eight to twelve.

Presentation
Teacher.

What you need
Pictures of athletes, especially runners; cuttings from the newspaper about marathons.
Songs 'For All the Strength We Have', *SSL*; 'Hands to Work and Feet to Run', *SSL*.

What to do
Explain the origin of the marathon. This long distance race commemorates the run from Marathon to Athens to announce the defeat of the Persians in 490 BC. It has been an Olympic event since 1896. The exact distance run is 42.195 km (26 miles 385 yds).

In recent years people have become more interested in sport and keeping fit, and there has been a corresponding growth in the number of local amateur marathons and half-marathons. Runners enjoy the challenge of completing such a long run or improving their time over the distance. Use the pictures to illustrate the fitness of athletes. Mention could be made of the many disabled participants in marathons, and of wheelchair marathons themselves.

Each year huge crowds participate in the London and Boston marathons. Focus on particular individuals who ran in the most recent marathon – you may know of some local participants. Emphasise the time and effort put into training for the marathon. The children might like to follow this up by organising their own long-distance run to raise funds.

A Victorian school day

Age range
Eight to twelve.

Presentation
Teacher and class.

What to do
This assembly could form the conclusion of a project on Victorian times. Parents and grandparents could be invited into school to talk about their schooling and be questioned by the children; this works particularly well if all have attended the same school, though this is rare nowadays. If possible, take the children to folk and other museums which provide examples of Victorian lifestyles. Many museums now run simulations of Victorian school life. Use this work to develop your own glimpse into a Victorian classroom, with the children and yourself playing appropriate roles and including examples of the type of work and discipline of the day. The children could dress up for the occasion. Present this drama sequence in the assembly and then discuss with the children the ways in which schools have changed in the last hundred years. Do they think that they have changed for the better?

The Children of Courage awards

Age range
Five to twelve.

Presentation
Teacher.

What you need
Try to obtain information on the latest Children of Courage awards sponsored by *Woman's Own*, or any local children who have received attention for acts of courage.
Prayers *LPT* 36; *WYP* 60.
Songs 'The Journey of Life', *CP SSL*; 'He Who Would Valiant Be', *CP*.

What to do
It isn't only grown-ups who help others, either by the example they set or a particular act. Every year a number of young people receive their Children of Courage awards for an act of bravery. Some cope courageously with physical or mental handicap or with pain as a result of an accident, illness or operation. Others are honoured because they perform some heroic act, like rescuing another person from danger. For example, in 1983 Sharon Pankhurst, aged ten, received the award for saving her brothers when their home in Leeds caught fire; she remained calm as flames swept through the rooms, dropping each of the boys – aged five, four, two and one – out of the window to her father 20 feet below. Only when they were safe did she jump herself.

Tell the children about any more examples that you have heard about. (John Craven's *Newsround* often covers the event; local newspapers are also a good source of stories.)

The building of the Bell Rock Lighthouse

Age range
Seven to twelve.

Presentation
Teacher.

What you need
A torch or lamp; pieces of dovetailed wood or card or a large jigsaw; a map of Scotland.
Songs 'Bobbing up and down like this', *OK*; 'When Lamps are Lighted in the Town', *SSL*; 'Whenever I Feel Afraid', *AP*.

What to do
Tell the children the story of how Robert Stevenson built the Bell Rock Lighthouse which stands at the entrance to the Firth of Forth in Scotland (indicate on the map). Explain how the rock was very dangerous to ships – but very hard to build on. When the tide was out, people could stand on the rock – but when the tide was in, it was 3.5 metres under water!

How could Stevenson and his workforce even begin to build a lighthouse? If they landed and laid some stones down, they would be washed away by the very next tide. They anchored two ships near the rock for the men to live on – and 67 men were able to work on the rock when the tide was out. Then Stevenson built a wooden platform on the rock itself. People could work there cutting and shaping the huge stones. The hardest part was to get started: each of the huge foundation stones was cut to fit into the rock, and into the stones next to it, like a huge jigsaw puzzle (use visual aids). So when the tide came in, and the men had to climb into their wooden tower, the sea couldn't wash the stones away.

It took two years to build the Bell Rock Lighthouse. And it's still there – the light flashing as a warning to ships as they come into the Firth of Forth. Use the torch to demonstrate the flashing light.

Market day

Age range
Eight to twelve.

Presentation
Teacher and class.

What you need
A range of items to put on market stalls.
Song 'Come Let us Remember the Joys of the Town', *SSL*.

What to do
Markets are exciting places, full of bustle and noise.
Most schools have some kind of weekly or daily market
in their local area. Prepare for the assembly by taking the
children to visit the market. Group the children and ask
each group to select a type of stall to observe. Back at
school, develop a situation drama based on a market
setting with the children setting up their own stalls. The TV
programme *EastEnders* is a further source of ideas.

Use the drama sequence as the focus of the assembly.
Explain that markets have been important places for
exchanging goods for hundreds of years. Most old towns
have a market square and the weekly markets also
provided an important social function — a chance to meet
other people and exchange news. Talk about the
development of the supermarket and how shopping has
become less of a social event (though some
hypermarkets now have coffee bars to encourage people
to linger and chat).

Tomorrow's world

Age range
Eight to twelve.

Presentation
Teacher.

What you need
A transistor radio, a quartz watch, a computer and any other interesting examples of modern technology; pictures of modern inventions, particularly any that are socially beneficial such as electronic wheelchairs or a miniature hearing aid.
Prayers *TAP*, nos 10, 11, 17, 42, 79.
Music 'Tubular Bells', Mike Oldfield; Theme from *Tomorrow's World*.

What to do
Turn on the transistor radio, alter the volume and stations. We take transistor radios for granted – they are relatively cheap and simple. Take the back off the radio and show the children the miniature components inside. Explain how the invention of the silicon chip has changed technology and allowed us to make things much smaller and more convenient. Compare the quartz watch and modern computer with their predecessors. Explain how the computer has radically changed our work environment, reducing the time taken to do jobs and the workforce required. Cars and other goods are now manufactured on robot assembly lines.

Can the children think of other ways that the computer and modern technology have affected our lives? Perhaps some of them have seen the latest developments on *Tomorrow's World* (BBC TV). What about the changes in the types of toys available – remote-control cars, video games etc?

Ask the children what they would like to invent if they had the knowledge and resources. Try to show that technology can be used in both positive and negative ways. Would their ideas be socially beneficial and what about the effects on the environment?

Stories from different cultures and religions

The family of man and woman

Age range
Eight to twelve.

Presentation
Teacher, representatives from different religions.

What you need
World Religions: a Handbook for Teachers, W Owen Cole, Commission for Racial Equality. *Man and his Gods, An Encyclopaedia of World Religions*, E G Parrinder (ed), Hamlyn; *The Muslim World; The Jewish World; The Hindu World*.
Songs 'The Family of Man', Spinners CP; 'Come and Join Us', NH.

What to do
Get your class to draw a tree representing the Family of man and woman; each branch representing a different religion and each leaf a person with his or her own individual thoughts and feelings. Choose one branch for each assembly and invite someone of each religion to come along to your school.

   Begin the assembly with 'Come and Join Us'; this can be used whenever the children are welcoming a guest. Then, using the chart, explain that each branch of the tree has important things in common with all the other branches. They all want to love and to be kind to other people and they all want good deeds to be done. Each branch has a different way of doing these things; the differences are exciting and stimulating. Follow with a short discussion and question session. Finally, the children can perform a prepared dramatisation of a traditional story.

Story-tellers

Age range
Seven to twelve.

Presentation
Parents or representatives from different cultural backgrounds who are willing to tell or read a story from their own particular folklore. *Listen to this Story* by Grace Hallworth, Magnet, for example, provides a wonderful selection of stories from the West Indies.

What to do
Establish contact with someone willing to tell/read a story from their cultural folklore. Ask them to introduce the story by telling the children about the country of origin, especially any personal anecdotes. With sufficient volunteers this could form the basis of a series of assemblies. Include some folk tales of your own choosing. Explain to the children that story-telling is an ancient tradition and that many stories have been passed down from generation to generation long before they were put into print.

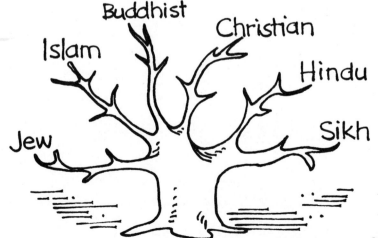

Texts from world religions

Age range
Eight to twelve.

Presentation
Teacher.

What you need
Stories of caring taken from a number of religions can be found in *Religion in the Multifaith School*, ed by W Owen Cole, Hulton Educational Publications 1983.

What to do
It is important, before presenting a selection of religious texts on the theme of caring, sharing and doing to others what we would like them to do to us, to consider the context in which they were written. They belong to a living community and words taken out of context can be dangerous. The book by W Owen Cole provides useful background information on world religions. The following extracts were selected by the editor, together with the names of the main holy books.

'The righteous man is he who gives his wealth to his kinfolk, to orphans, to the needy, to wayfarers and beggars and the redemption of prisoners.'

Buddhism To give alms, to live religiously, to protect relatives, to perform blameless deeds, this is true blessedness (*Dhammapada* and *Lotus Sutra*). To wait on mother and father, to cherish child and wife and follow a quiet calling, this is true blessedness. Embrace friendliness for the whole world (*Three Baskets/Tripataka*).

Christianity Jesus said, 'As much as you do it to the least of my little ones, you do it to me'.

Confucius Never do to others what you would not like them to do to you. Show piety towards your parents and kindness towards your children.

Hinduism No guest must stay in your house without being honoured according to your ability to do so, by being given a seat, food, a couch, water, vegetables or fruit (*Vedas, Upanishads*). Ahimsa does not simply mean non-killing. Himsa means causing pain to or killing any life out of anger, or from a selfish purpose, or with the intention of injuring it. Refraining from so doing is Ahimsa (*Bhagavad Gita*).

Islam The righteous man is he who gives his wealth to his kinsfolk, to orphans, to the needy, to wayfarers and beggars, and the redemption of prisoners (*Qur'an*). Show kindness to parents, to relatives, orphans and the poor, to the person under your care whether he is your relative or not, and to the companion at your side.

Jainism This is the duty of a true man — to shelter all, as a tree provides shade in the fierce sun, and to labour so that many men enjoy what he earns, as the fruit of a fertile tree.

Judaism Seek justice, relieve the oppressed, help the fatherless to obtain justice, plead for the widow. What does the Lord require of you but to do justice, to love mercy, and to walk humbly with your God (*Talmud, Mishnah*).

Parsism He who supports the helpless poor acknowledges the kingdom of God.

In the beginning – an African tale

Age range
Eight to twelve.

Presentation
Teacher.

What you need
A world globe.
Music Missa Luba (*LVRI/LLST757*).

What to do
Explain to the children that for centuries, all over the world, people have been fascinated by the possible origins of the human race, and that there are all sorts of stories told by different cultures.

Show the children the globe and ask if anyone can find the continent of Africa. Tell the children about the remains of primitive people that have been found in parts of Africa.

In Africa, many tribes have their own stories about how things began. The Shilluk people, who live on the White Nile, tell of the way in which their god, Juok, created humankind. 'I will make people to live on the earth,' said Juok to himself. 'I will form them out of the soil of the lands where they are to live.' So Juok went to the northern country where the land stretched white and sandy. 'Here I will make white people,' said Juok. Then he came to the country of Egypt, where the great River Nile flooded its wide valley to make fields of good brown soil. 'In this place I will make brown men and women,' said Juok.

Then he travelled up the Nile towards the lakes and marshes where the Shilluk now live, and where the earth is fine and black. Juok smiled. 'Here I will make black people to be like their rich soil.' And so Juok made humankind in different colours according to the land on which they lived, and from which they get their food. 'White, brown, black,' said Juok, 'and to each I give two arms, two eyes, two ears and one mouth. Then they can all dig the fields, see the plants grow, hear the sounds of speech and sing with joy.'

And Juok was happy with all the people that he had made.

Dreamtime

Age range
Eight to twelve.

Presentation
Teacher.

What you need
A world globe.

What you do
Explain to the children that you are going to read to them a story that the Aborigines, who now live in Australia, tell to explain how things were created. This story could be linked with the African creation story on page 83.

We have been told, as our fathers were before us, that there was land, but it was a bare, flat, barren plain. No animals ran there. No birds sang overhead. No trees or bushes grew. No sound of water could be heard. Nor was there any man or woman.

Baiame, or the Maker of Many Things as some call him, brought the Dreamtime ancestors from under the ground and over the seas. With them, life came to the barren, flat plain. Some of the Dreamtime ancestors looked like men or women. Others looked like the animals or creatures which descended from them. But often the Dreamtime ancestors could change their shape. So the Swordfish ancestor could look like a swordfish, or a man or woman.

As the Dreamtime ancestors wandered over the land, many adventures befell them. They met with other ancestors. Arguments often arose, and the ancestors would set out on their travels again. They met strange creatures and fought battles. Each time something happened, the very shape of the land changed. Hills arose, plants grew. Where the Barramundi-fish ancestor swam, rivers appeared. When people, ancestors or animals did what they should not, the Rainbow Snake would rush down upon them. He would either drown them, making bays or rivers, or swallow them. Then he would spit out their bones to form rocks and hills. But the Rainbow Snake is not just vengeful. To some peoples, the Rainbow Snake is Old Woman, who in Dreamtime taught her children – humans – to talk and understand. She also taught them how to dig for food, and what to eat.

And the sun, moon and the stars? These also came to be in the Dreamtime. For one day, Emu ancestor and Eagle ancestor were fighting. Eagle took one of Emu's eggs, and threw it into the air. Soaring up, it burst into flames. Baiame fed the flame with wood. So the sun was made, and is made anew each day with fresh wood.

The Dreamtime ancestors taught their groups how to perform secret ceremonies. Then the ancestors sank back into the earth or rose into the sky, but remain ever present.

But Dreamtime is not over. For when ceremonies are performed, Dreamtime comes to those who celebrate, and they learn to see this land as the Dreaming sees it – alive.

Confucius and friends

Age range
Seven to twelve.

Presentation
Teacher.

What you need
Any Chinese artifacts – paintings, clothes, a wok, a kite etc.

What to do
Show the artifacts to the children and ask if they know which country the artifacts come from. China is a country which, since ancient times, has produced some beautiful art and literature. Explain to the children that you are going to tell them a very old story from China.

Many hundreds of years ago, there lived in China a man called K'Ung Fu'Tzu. We know him as Confucius. He was very wise and he became a special adviser or minister to one of the great rulers of the country. So great was his wisdom and so useful was his advice that he became very famous and very popular.

Indeed, he became so popular and so famous that the ruler grew jealous. 'Confucius,' he said to himself, 'Confucius must go.' And so Confucius had to go.

With a few friends, Confucius started to travel round the country, teaching the people he met. And what did he teach? He said this: 'What you do not like when it is done to you, do not do to others.'

Once, he met a hermit – someone who hides away and wants nothing to do with people.

'Huh,' said the hermit, 'You're wasting your time. People are mean. People are cruel. You're wasting your time, trying to teach them to be good. You're stupid.'

And Confucius said, 'To have people be rude to you and not to mind, that is the wise way.'

And later, to his friends, he said, 'We should do good to others whether we need to or not.'

His friends all learned a great deal from Confucius. One of them, Tseng Tzu, learned this: 'Every night, I ask myself three things. In what I have done for others today, have I done my best? To my friends, have I been loyal and true? And have I told others to do only what I would do myself? If so, I have been a good friend.'

The signs of Sikhism

Age range
Eight to twelve.

Presentation
Teacher.

What you need
I am a Sikh, Franklin Watts; *The Sikh World*, Macdonald.

Objects or pictures to represent the five Ks: Kara, a steel bangle (symbolising the unity of God); Kanga, a comb; Kesh, uncut hair; Kirpan, a sword or dagger; Kaccha, under-shorts.

What to do
The five Ks are the most significant symbols in the daily lives of Sikhs. Tell the children the story from which the symbols originated.

The tenth Guru, or Great Teacher, was Guru Gobind Singh. In 1699 he founded the Khalsa, the brotherhood of Sikhs, because at that time Sikhs were being persecuted. At the April festival of Baisakhi, the Guru asked a gathering of Sikhs if any of them were willing to die for their faith. Five men agreed. The Guru took the first one away and soon returned with a blood-stained sword. Even though they believed the first man to be dead, the other four still went out with the Guru. Then he returned with all of them alive. He made them members of the Khalsa, gave them the new name 'Singh' (meaning lion), and told them to wear the five Ks, symbols of their membership – as illustrated.

The Kirpan may be a tiny ornamental one on the Kara. The turban is not one of the Ks, but a neat way of retaining the Kesh. Not all Sikhs belong to the Khalsa, but many do.

The Japji Sahib is a prayer which speaks of God who makes and controls all things. It is often called 'The Morning Prayer'. The introduction to it sums up Sikh belief in God.
There is one God,
Everlasting truth is His name;
He is the maker of all things;
He is present in all things;
He fears nothing
And He is against nothing.

The story of Mahagiri

Age range
Five to eight.

Presentation
Teacher.

What you need
For the story of Mahagiri see opposite. Pictures of elephants – both Indian and African; a wood carving of an Indian elephant.
Music *Carnival of the Animals*, Saint-Saens, available as a Scholastic cassette.

What to do
Ask the children if any of them have ever seen an elephant. Can they describe one? Perhaps they can estimate how much an elephant weighs. Do they know the difference between an African and an Indian elephant?

Explain that although elephants are huge animals they are not aggressive and are often used as domestic animals. What type of jobs do the children think they might do? Unfortunately, although elephants do not harm people they are sometimes killed. Do the children know why? Explain that some people think that the tusks have magical and medicinal properties and that the elephant is now a protected species.

Tell the story of Mahagiri. Point out how gentle the elephant was. Why did the people get angry with Mahagiri? What do the children think they should have done?

Elephants work hard in India. One elephant who worked very hard indeed was Mahagiri. His master would send him with his mahout into the forest to move heavy logs of wood, to lead the temple procession at festival time, or to carry very important people in the howdah on his back. The children all knew him, of course, but were always rather afraid of the elephant.

One day, Mahagiri was sent to a village to do the kind of job he enjoyed most. The people wanted to put up their new flag outside the temple for a festival, but they had no flag pole. The villagers had found a good, straight tree in the jungle and cut it down. It was too heavy for anyone except Mahagiri to lift.

Steadily he carried it back to the village. The hole was ready in front of the temple. Suddenly, as he came to the hole, Mahagiri stopped and turned away. The mahout ordered Mahagiri to put the flag pole into the hole, but the elephant did not move. Again and again he told Mahagiri what to do but still he did not move. The mahout beat Mahagiri with his stick but it made no difference. He threw down the flag pole and bellowed very loudly. The mahout ws thrown off and the people all ran away in fear of this wild, mad elephant.

Mahagiri was quite alone. He went to the hole and knelt down. Slowly, he stretched his long trunk into the hole and picked up a tiny, shivering kitten. It had been hiding in the hole.

The people of the village, who had been peeping round far-off corners, knew now why Mahagiri had refused to do as his mahout had told him. He had not wanted to hurt the little kitten. They ran to him and cheered as he lifted the flag pole into the hole and held it still while they filled the hole with earth. Everyone patted Mahagiri and said 'Well done!'
* Adapted from *Mahagiri* by Hemalata, Children's Book Trust in India.

Games around the world

Age range
Six to twelve.

Presentation
Teacher and children.

What you need
Games around the world, a pack of 40 games available from UNICEF.
Prayer *LBCP*, page 22.

What to do
Teach the children some of the games from the pack. Try to include various types – team games, ball games, board games etc. The children can demonstrate the games and, using a world map, point to the countries of their origins.

Ask the children about the games that they like to play in the playground. Are there any similarities between these and the games played by children in other countries? Point out that all the games demonstrated cost nothing to play since no expensive or elaborate materials are needed.

Networks
The Shongo tribe children of Zaire live in small villages where there are no toy stores. They enjoy creating their own games such as Networks.

The idea is to draw a pattern or figure in the sand using one continuous line. You cannot go back over a line. If you have to lift your finger to finish the pattern, you have made a mistake. Try to finish your pattern in more than one way.

You can play Networks with your friends. See how many patterns you can draw, and who finishes a pattern first.

The fish spear
1 Put the string over the thumbs and little fingers of both hands.

2 With your right index finger, pick up the string which runs across your left palm and pull it out a little.

3 Twist it by twirling your right index finger around this string three times. Now pull the figure tight by extending your hands.

4 Reach your left index finger down through the loop which is on your right index finger, and pick up the string which runs across the right palm. Pull this string back through the loop.

5 Pull the figure tight again.

6 Release the loops from your right thumb and little finger, and there is the fish spear.

Clap ball

This game is played by boys and girls in Cameroon, a country near the equator in Africa. Cameroon children often use clapping and rhythms in their games. Clap ball is a perfect example of this.

To play, you need a round fruit, like an orange or grapefruit, or a small rubber ball. You can play on any size of field. A straight line is drawn down the centre of the field and two teams are formed.

The members of each team stand six feet away from the centre line on their side of the field.

The first player throws the ball to any player on the other team. All the players clap once as he throws. When the ball is caught, they stamp their feet. The catcher throws the ball to someone on the other side, and all players clap and stamp as before. This repeats over and over.

Both teams must stay off the dividing line. If a player misses a throw, he returns the ball to the thrower, who throws it to him again. No one wins or loses in this lively game; it is played just for the enjoyment of the rhythm.

Fire on the mountain

Boys and girls can play this Tanzanian game. Any number of players and a leader are needed.

All the players lie on their backs. They choose any word or name to be the 'key word'. When the leader calls out the key word, all the players have to stand up quickly.

The game starts when the leader shouts 'Fire on the mountain!' All the players answer 'Fire!' but do not jump up. Then the leader shouts 'Fire on the river!' Again the players answer 'Fire!' but do not jump up. This goes on. Each time the leader says 'Fire on the . . .,' he changes the last word of the phrase. He tries to think of many different places for the fire.

The leader can shout the key word at any time, between the phrases or in the middle of them. When he does, the player who jumps up last is out of the game.

The player who stays in the game the longest is the winner.

The wounded swan

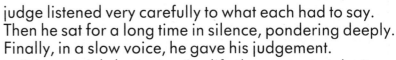

Age range
Eight to twelve.

Presentation
Teacher.

What to do
Read the children this story of the Buddha's boyhood. The Buddha, or Siddhartha Gautama, was born in northern India about 2,500 years ago. When he was a baby, a wise man predicted that Siddhartha Gautama would either become a great emperor or a great religious teacher. His father, King Suddhodana, wanted an heir to follow him on the throne of his kingdom when he died. So, in order that his son's mind did not turn in the direction of religious things, he kept him in luxurious palaces while he was growing up. But even so, Siddhartha showed great compassion. This story tells of an argument he had with his cousin Devadatta, who was always his rival, and who plotted against him when they were older.

One day, while Prince Siddhartha was exploring the palace grounds, a beautiful white swan fell wounded at his feet. Someone had shot it with an arrow! Stooping down, Siddhartha pulled the arrow out very gently. Then he soothed the poor, frightened bird until it fell asleep, cradled in his arms.

Suddenly his cousin, Devadetta, came bursting out of the bushes. He was carrying a bow.

'Aha, there's my bird. Give her to me at once,' he demanded.

But Siddhartha would not let Devadetta take the swan and kill it. So, after a long argument, the two boys agreed to ask a wise judge to decide the matter for them. The judge listened very carefully to what each had to say. Then he sat for a long time in silence, pondering deeply. Finally, in a slow voice, he gave his judgement.

'It is certainly better to give life than to try to take it away. This bird must therefore belong to the boy who tried to save its life, not to he who tried to kill it.' And he told Siddhartha that the swan was his.

Siddhartha nursed that swan with great gentleness and care. And when it was better, he let it go free.

When they have heard the story, ask the children to think about whether the judge was right, and whether Siddhartha should have been allowed to keep the wounded swan. Should Devadatta have been given the bird? The children could also think or talk about other people who nursed animals and birds back to health and strength.

The dove with the olive leaf

Age range
Five to twelve.

Presentation
Teacher.

What you need
A large illustration of a dove carrying an olive branch.
Hymn 'Morning has Broken', *CP*.
Prayer *LBCP* 43.

What to do
Remind the children of the story of Noah. Explain that Noah in the ark had no signs to follow. All around was nothing but water and sky. When it stopped raining after 40 days, water covered everything – even

mountains. A wind blew and the ark moved over the waves but no one knew where it was going. It drifted for 150 days. Then came a bump; the ark shuddered and stopped. It had come to rest on the top of a mountain.

Noah wondered if the danger was over and if the water was going down, so he sent out a dove. She flew round in a wide circle and came back to rest on his hand; she could see only water everywhere and nowhere to rest her feet. After seven days Noah sent her out again. This time she flew out of sight and when she came back she had an olive leaf in her beak. Then Noah knew that somewhere leaves were green again. The next time he sent out the dove she didn't come back at all, so he knew that she had found food and a place to build her nest.

Explain that the olive leaf was a sign that peace and happiness were coming back to the world after the terrible storms and the flood. To Noah it was like a green light saying, 'Go ashore – it's safe again'. Tell the children too that the dove has become a symbol of peace and happiness.

The mouse and the crow

Age range
Eight to twelve.

Presentation
Teacher.

What to do
Use this Indian tale, rewritten by John Snelling, to stress that in every culture and every religion, friends and friendships are very important.

One day in India, a crow happened to see a tiny mouse save an entire flock of doves by gnawing through a net in

which a hunter had caught them. The mouse did this because the leader of the doves was a good friend.

This impressed the crow so much that later, he called down to the mouse that he, too, wanted to be his friend.

'A crow? My friend?' the mouse called back. 'Crows eat mice, so how can we be friends? Be off with you, you black bandit.'

'Well, if you won't be my friend, I'll starve myself to death right here outside your hole,' the disappointed crow replied.

'But we are enemies – Nature made us that way!' the mouse protested.

'Listen. Up until now, we've never properly met each other,' the crow went on. 'When old enemies actually meet face to face, each often finds that the other isn't as bad as he thought. In fact they sometimes even get to like each other!'

They went on discussing the matter for ages. Eventually, the mouse was so impressed by the crow's good sense that he decided he could probably be trusted, so he popped his head out of the hole.

After that, they really did become good friends. Almost daily they would bring each other presents.

And then, one summer, there was a terrible drought. Both of them would certainly have died if the crow hadn't been able to fly carrying his tiny friend to another area where there was plenty of water.

Round the year . . .

The year ahead

Age range
Eight to twelve.

Presentation
Teacher.

What you need
A large year planner wallchart.
Books *Here's the Year*, Peter Watkins & Erica Hughes, Julia MacRae Books/Franklin Watts; *This Month, Next Month*, CIO; *The Months of the Year*, Paul Hughes, Young Library Ltd; *Something to Do*, Septima, Young Puffin; *Festivals*, Ruth Manning Saunders, Heinemann.
Songs 'Turn, turn, turn', *ST*; 'Days of the months', *HQ*.

What to do
An assembly for the start of the Spring term. A good time of year to take a look ahead and gain an overall impression of the changing seasons and the months to come. Introduce each month by explaining the origin of the name and, with the children's help, fill in any major events, festivals etc on the year planner. (See calendar of festivals and events in the appendix.) Note that not all New Year celebrations occur in January.

January – Named after the Roman god Janus. Janus had two faces, one facing backwards into the old year and the other facing forwards into the new year.
February – The origin of the name is uncertain – either named after Februus, the Roman god of purification, or after a februa, a musical instrument.
March – This month is named after Mars, the Roman god of war, crops and vegetation.

April – The name is believed to have come from the Latin word 'aperire', which means 'to open'. This is because in the Northern Hemisphere buds start to open and plants begin to grow during April.
May – May is named after either Maia, the Greek goddess, or Maia Majesta, the Italian goddess of spring.
June – Once again there are two possible origins of the name – either Junius, the name of an old Roman tribe or Juno, the Roman goddess who was the wife of Jupiter.
July – In the Roman calendar this month was originally called 'Quintilius', as it was their fifth month (the Roman calendar started in March). However, it was later changed to Julius, in honour of Julius Cæsar.
August – The original Roman name, 'Sextilis', (sixth month), was changed to 'Augustus' in honour of the Roman emperor Augustus Cæsar.
September – The seventh month in the Roman calendar, the original name 'Septem', meaning seven, was retained and hence the origin of September.
October – October comes from the Roman word 'octo', meaning eight, as it was the eighth month in the old Roman calendar.
November – This comes from the Roman word 'novem', meaning nine.
December – Used to be the tenth month of the Roman calendar and therefore named 'Decem', which means ten.

Valentine's Day

Age range
Five to twelve.

Presentation
Teacher.

What you need
Valentine cards, both manufactured and produced by the children. If possible, include some pictures of Victorian Valentine cards.
Prayer *TWI* , no 20.
Song 'Love Is Something If You Give It Away', *NO*.

What to do
It is the tradition on St Valentine's Day to send cards to those you love. This custom originates from the Roman festival of love when young people chose their sweethearts by drawing lots. St Valentine was a priest who lived in Rome and was killed in AD 270 for giving shelter to Christians. As his death coincided with the festival of love, the association was established.

Ask the children if any of them sent or will be sending cards. Look at some of the cards on display and read out the greetings. Why is it important to show people that you love them and care about them? Ask the children for suggestions and write them down on a blackboard. Widen the topic to include concern for others or other occasions when we send greetings cards to make people happy.

Spring growth

Age range
Seven to twelve.

Presentation
Teacher and class.

What you need
Poem 'The Fight of the Year', Roger McGough.
Prayers *LBCP* 16.
Songs 'Who Put the Colours in the Rainbow?', *CP*; 'Song of Life', *ECS*; 'This Joyful Eastertide', *MFC*.

What to do
Use the poem to illustrate the theme of growth and new life during the Easter term. The whole class could recite the poem with individual children calling out the items in the list sections whilst holding up paintings to illustrate these.

If your school has a garden the children could talk about what is already growing and what other plants and seeds they are planning to put in during the springtime.

The Fight of the Year
'And there goes the bell for the third month
and Winter comes out of its corner looking groggy
Spring leads with a left to the head
followed by a sharp right to the body
   daffodils

primroses
crocuses
snowdrops
lilacs
violets
pussywillow
Winter can't take much more punishment
and Spring shows no signs of tiring
   tadpoles
   squirrels
   baa-lambs
   bunny rabbits
   mad march hares
   horses and hound
Spring is merciless.

Winter won't go the full twelve rounds
   bob tail clouds
   scally-waggy winds
   the sun
   a pavement artist
   in every town
A left to the chin
and Winter's down!
   1) tomatoes
   2) radish
   3) cucumber
   4) onions
   5) beetroot
   6) celery
   7) and any
   8) amount
   9) of lettuce
  10) for dinner
Winter's out for the count
Spring is the winner!'

All Fools' Day

Age range
Seven to twelve.

Presentation
Teacher.

What you need
Some foolish ideas!

What to do
Prepare your own April Fool for the children; some dramatic (but not too disturbing) change to school policy. For example, you could announce that you have just received a circular that has been sent out to all schools in the country instructing them to abolish playtimes. It is felt that these are an unnecessary waste of time! You and the staff realise this will be most disappointing for the children but there is nothing that you can do. However, in order for the staff to have a coffee break you have decided to hold an assembly each day during the breaktime. The more you can elaborate, the better.

   Finally, look as if you are about to finish the assembly and announce, 'April Fools to you children', and wait for the response!

May Day

Age range
Seven to twelve.

Presentation
Teacher and children.

What you need
A maypole; coloured tissue paper to make flowers or well-dressings.
Song 'Sing a Song of Maytime', NCS; 'May song', GY.

What to do
Tell the children about the traditions of May Day. This is the first day in May and is a public holiday in many countries. In Britain the national holiday is on the first Monday of the month. This is also known as Labour Day, when we remember the efforts of working men and women around the world. May Day is an ancient festival and traditionally fairs were held in every town and village. Early on May Day morning young people would go and gather greenery and May blossom for decorations. It was also believed that bathing in the fresh dew of the morning would ensure everlasting beauty.

The maypole formed the central part of May Day customs – decorated with colourful ribbons and flowers. If you have a maypole in school, a group of children could perform some dances or, alternatively, you may be able to persuade some morris dancers to provide a performance for the children.

In Celtic times May Day marked the beginning of summer when cattle, which had been brought down from the hills in November, were taken back to the upland pastures.

Let the children decorate the hall with paper flowers. They could also make well-dressings, using paper petals – in Derbyshire, at this time of year, people have traditionally decorated the ancient sources of water with magnificent pictures made out of flower petals.

World Children's Day

Age range
Eight to twelve.

Presentation
Teacher and class.

What you need
Information on children and everyday life in other countries can be obtained from embassies, Oxfam, Save The Children Fund, UNICEF, the World Development Movement and the Commonwealth Institute (addresses on pages 124 and 125).
Prayer *LPT* 26.
Song 'He's Got the Whole World in his Hands', *CP*.

What to do
In Britain World Children's Day is June 15. Nearly 50 per cent of the world's population is made up of children under 15. A large proportion of these children are in a state of suffering, so the United Nations General Assembly decided to set aside one special day each year for children around the world. On that day we think of children from all parts of the globe, especially those who do not enjoy the same standard of living as ourselves.

   Before the assembly, split your class into small groups and ask each group to find out about what life would be like for children of a similar age in selected parts of the world. Information from charitable organisations often provides profiles on particular children. Each group could then produce an account of 'A day in the life of . . .', with supporting illustrations, and these could be presented in the assembly.

St Swithin's Day

Age range
Seven to twelve.

Presentation
Teacher.

What to do
If it rains on St Swithin's Day (15 July) then the next 40 days are likely to be wet too. That's the old wives' tale based on an event that took place in the ninth century. Tell the children the background to the superstition.

St Swithin, the much loved Bishop of Winchester at that time, disliked pomp and humbly requested that when he died he should be buried outside the cathedral, so that everyone who came to worship would walk on his grave.

His wish was granted for a while – but when the monks moved his body from the common graveyard back into Winchester Cathedral, apparently it rained for 40 days and everyone assumed that St Swithin disapproved.

When it does rain on July 15, country people often say that St Swithin is 'christening the apples'. This simple saying is well-known in rural areas.

'St Swithin's Day, if thou dost rain,
For forty days it will remain.
St Swithin's Day, if thou be fair,
For forty days' twill rain no more.'

Ask the children if they know of any other old wives' tales or superstitions, eg red sky at night, shepherd's delight, red sky in the morning, shepherd's warning. Do they think these sayings have any factual origins? A group of children could keep a rain chart to see how much it does rain after St Swithin's Day.

Back from the holidays

Age range
Five to eight.

Presentation
Teacher.

What you need
Anything interesting that you found or bought on your own holiday.
Music 'Summer Holiday', Cliff Richard on 'More Hits by Cliff Richard'.
Song 'Oh, I Do Like to be Beside the Seaside', *TB*.

What to do
This assembly could be held at the beginning of any term but is best held at the beginning of the school year. Welcome the children back to school. Talk about the strange feeling we all experience when we come back to school after a long break – a real shock to the system! Do they have difficulty remembering where they've put things, find it difficult to get going again in the mornings or find they can't remember people's names? The children will also have some anxieties about going into a new class, the new teacher and what they will be expected to do.

However, this can also be an exciting time – meeting old friends again, catching up on each other's news etc. Tell the children about some of the things that you did in the holidays – visiting new places; seeing your relatives; pursuing your favourite hobby and so on. Try to think of an amusing tale to tell or bring something that tells a story of its own. Invite the children to join in and share some of their own holiday experiences.

A bumper harvest

Age range
Five to seven.

Presentation
Teacher and a few volunteers.

What you need
A wide variety of fruits and vegetables. If possible produce from the school garden could be harvested for the occasion. An artificial enormous turnip made from a white sheet stuffed with newspaper and topped with crêpe-paper leaves. This should be hidden in a box covered with brown paper to represent the soil.
Hymn 'First the Seed', *NCS*.
Prayer *LPT*, page 13.

What to do
Show the children the fruits and vegetables and see if they can name them and tell which part of the world they come from. Talk about how they are grown and how they need to be cared for properly if they are to bear fruit. Ask the children to tell you about any plants or seeds that they have grown themselves. Point out how patient you have to be when growing things, but how exciting it is when they eventually reach the stage when you can harvest them.

Now tell the story of the Enormous Turnip and invite the children to take part as the story develops. At the climax of the story help them to heave the enormous turnip out of the box.

Hallowe'en

Age range
Five to twelve.

Presentation
Teacher.

What you need
Music *The Sorcerer's Apprentice*, Paul Dukas.
Song 'Hallowe'en's coming', *HQ*.
Stories *Witches*, C Rawson, Usborne Books; *It's Hallowe'en*, J Prelutsky, World's Work; *Simon and the Witch*, M Stuart Barry, Armada Lions; *A Witch in the Family*, Z K Snyder, Beaver; *The Witch's Garden*, L Postma, Hutchinson.

What to do
Hallowe'en, or All Hallows' Eve, is the night before All Saints' Day and is celebrated on October 31. It marks the end of autumn and the beginning of winter and used to be a new year celebration. People believed that in the time of transition from the old to the new year there were many spirits around. Light was an important force used to ward off evil spirits, hence the tradition of Hallowe'en lanterns.

These days it is often the occasion of 'Trick or Treat' where neighbourbood children visit houses and demand a treat to avoid the playing of a trick. Some people can react negatively to Hallowe'en and treatment of the festival should be handled sensitively.

Explain to the children that in the past, if people could not explain an event they attributed it to magic and witchcraft. Nowadays, although we no longer believe in witches, fairies, hobgoblins, and other magic folk, we can still enjoy listening to stories about them. Read the children a story or extract from a book suitable for the age group involved.

Invite some of the children to demonstrate some Hallowe'en customs, such as apple-bobbing or dropping candle wax in water to form an image of your true love. A group of children could make some turnip and pumpkin lanterns prior to the assembly and these could be lit to demonstrate the power of light over darkness and evil.

Remembrance Sunday

Age range
Five to eleven.

Presentation
Teacher.

What you need
Poppies for sale during the week prior to Remembrance Sunday; a wall planner, diary, address book and some memento that you have which reminds you of an old friend or relative.
Music 'Imagine', John Lennon.

What to do
Select a few children and ask them if they can remember what they were doing this time yesterday; a week ago; a year ago. See how far back they can remember, especially for occasions like birthdays. Why do we remember some things and not others? Their specific memories should illustrate that we remember things that are important to us, including both sad and happy events.

What do we do to help us remember things? Talk about how we write memos, make shopping lists, tie a knot in a hanky etc. Show the children the wall planner, the diary and the address book and explain how they help us to remember. Show them your memento and tell the children something special that you remember about your friend/relative.

Go on to explain that Remembrance Sunday is a day when we remember all the people killed in the two world wars. We use the poppy as a symbol to remember them by because there were a lot of poppies growing in the fields in Flanders where many soldiers died. Emphasise the horror of war and how remembering the people who died makes us realise how important it is to keep peace in our time.

Winter

Age range
Five to twelve.

Presentation
Teacher.

What you need
A selection of appropriate and inappropriate clothing for winter weather.

Music Theme from *The Snowman*; Winter movement from Vivaldi's *The Four Seasons*; Sleigh Ride; Winter Wonderland.

Prayer *LBCP* page 44, *TWI* no 60.

Songs 'See How the Snowflakes are Falling', *SSL*; 'Snowflakes', *HQ*; 'Ho! Jack Frost', *HQ*.

Story 'The Snow Queen', Hans Christian Andersen.

What to do
Hold this assembly on a cold, preferably snowy day. Start the assembly by giving the children a really grim weather forecast – snow blizzards, freezing temperatures, icy roads and so on. What do they think about weather like that? Is it terrible or fun, or a bit of both? Why do they enjoy/not enjoy snow and ice? What happens to our environment when it snows – what does it look like, feel like, sound like? How do people cope with the bad weather? Talk about the problems of burst waterpipes, icy roads and pavements, disruption to transport and the ways that we try to overcome these difficulties. Why is it not much fun for old people? Do the children know any old people that they can keep an eye on during cold weather?

Ask for volunteers to help you select some suitable clothing to wear in cold, wet, winter weather. Choose a 'model' to dress and discuss the importance of keeping warm and dry – watch that heat loss from your head! You could also talk about how animals and birds cope in the winter.

Festivals

Eid-ul-Fitr

Age range
Five to twelve.

Presentation
Teacher and children.

What you need
I am a Muslim, Franklin Watts; *Gifts and Almonds*, Joan Solomon, Hamish Hamilton.

What to do
Eid-ul-Fitr is the Muslim festival which marks the end of Ramadan. Ramadan is a month of fasting when Muslims do not eat between dawn and dusk (excluding the elderly, the sick and children under ten). This abstinence helps Muslims to be aware of and appreciate the gifts which God has given to them. The Islamic year is a lunar one so the exact date for the beginning of Ramadan needs to be checked each year.

The festival of Eid-ul-Fitr lasts for three days and is a time for celebration after the fast. It is a particularly exciting time for children since they are given presents. People wear new clothes and sometimes decorate their hands with a special dye. Greetings cards with the message 'Eid Mubarick' (Blessed Festival) are sent to friends. People exchange gifts of sweets, usually sugared almonds or Badam Burfi (sweet almond cakes).

Children could make Eid cards to mark the event and Muslim children could talk about the presents and family celebrations, and possibly demonstrate how to make some sweet almond cakes. The story 'Gifts and Almonds' tells of one family's celebration of Eid.

Carnival time

Age range
Five to twelve.

Presentation
A class event or involving the whole school.

What you need
Carnival Frieze A McKenzie available from Ujamaa Centre, Oxfam Education Department, 14 Brixton Road, London, SW9.
Song 'Everyone loves Carnival Night', *TB*.

What to do
Carnivals are folk festivals, a time when people dress up in national costume and other festive gear and perform traditional dances, plays and music. West Indian festivals are particularly well-known for their fun and gaiety and the lively music of the steel bands. Most carnivals take place in the period before Lent – a time of merriment and feasting preceding the time for fasting and abstinence.

Initiate your own school carnival time, either before Lent or in connection with some local folklore. Use this local folklore to devise songs, music and plays for the children to perform. This could be the time to start a school band – how about some old dustbins!

Chinese New Year

Age range
Five to eight.

Presentation
Teacher and children.

What you need
Chinese New Year Pack produced by the Minority Group Support Service, Southfields School, Coventry. This has the story of how the years got their names along with instructions for making lanterns, cards, posters and masks.
Song *HQ 24*.

Background
This festival falls some time between January and February. It lasts for 15 days and ends with Teng Chieh, the Lantern Festival. Preparations begin as the year draws to a close – cleaning houses, buying new clothes and cooking special foods.

New Year's Day is a very happy occasion. Incense, firecrackers, 'lucky' money given in red envelopes, flowers, lanterns and sweets are all a part of the day.

Each new year has the name of an animal (they recur every 12 years – see opposite). The most important is the dragon. This is considered a year of good fortune.

The festival ends 14 days later on the first full moon of the new year. Lanterns are made and lit, then carried in a procession. Again there are fireworks, music, bands etc.

The dragon (a symbol of good luck) for the procession is made of paper, silk and bamboo and can be 100 metres long. People hang gifts for the dragon out of upstairs windows and the dragon reaches up to get them – sometimes standing six men high.

What to do
Make masks of animals, kites, even a dragon and mime or do dance/drama of the story of the names of the year. Make dragon models, lanterns, cards and posters. Explore the theme of generosity and giving and wishes for prosperity and peace for the new year.

Happy New Year in Chinese is Kungshi Fa Ts'ai (pronounced koong-hay-fa-choy). Talk about turning over a new leaf at the start of a new year and making resolutions. The children could read out some of their own resolutions.

Chinese twelve year cycle
1972, 1984–Rat (or mouse)
1973, 1985–Bull
1974, 1986–Tiger
1975, 1987–Rabbit (or hare)
1976, 1988–Dragon
1977, 1989–Snake
1978, 1990–Horse
1979, 1991–Goat (or sheep)
1980, 1992–Monkey
1981, 1993–Cockerel
1982, 1994–Dog
1983, 1995–Pig (or boar)

Pancake day

Age range
Five to eight.

Presentation
Teacher and some children to help with the cooking.

What you need
Ingredients and equipment for making pancakes.

What to do
Not for the faint-hearted this! A very successful assembly requiring only a little preparation but a certain amount of expertise. Weigh out the ingredients for making a pancake and set up a portable Gaz stove or similar. Enlist the help of children to take charge of various ingredients and help stir the mixture. Whilst you are mixing the batter the children could all join in chanting:

> Mix a pancake, stir a pancake,
> Pop it in a pan.
> Fry a pancake, toss a pancake,
> Catch it if you can.　　　　Christina Rosetti

If you're competent, end by tossing the pancake.

Explain that people used to use up all their cream, eggs and fat before Lent since they would not be needing them for the next forty days. During Lent no luxury foods were eaten and sometimes people lived on just bread and water to remind themselves of how Jesus fasted in the wilderness before going out to teach.

Pesach: the feast of the Passover

Age range
Seven to twelve.

Presentation
Teacher and children.

What you need
Jewish Festivals, Reuben Turner, Wayland; *Festivals*, Jeanne McFarland, Macdonald Educational; *I am a Jew*, Franklin Watts.

What to do
This is the most important Jewish festival. It is a time when Jews remember how God freed the Jews from slavery in Egypt. Many years ago the Jews (Israelites) had to work as slaves for the Pharaohs of Egypt. Moses, their leader, pleaded with Pharaoh to let his people go but only after the Egyptians had a series of plagues inflicted on them did Pharaoh allow the Israelites to leave. They left very quickly before Pharaoh had a chance to change his mind.

A special Passover meal (the Seder) is eaten to mark the event. Roast shank of lamb is eaten in memory of the lamb sacrificed at the temple; bitter herbs as a reminder of suffering; Charoset, a sweet dish, to symbolise the joy of being set free; a bowl of salt water reminds them of the tears shed during the flight from Egypt and a roasted egg reminds people of the new life they are entering. Matzoh, unleavened bread, is eaten as an accompaniment to the meal. This is a reminder of the speed with which the Israelites left Egypt, allowing no time for their bread to rise.

Prepare a mock Passover meal with the children. During the assembly the children can sit round the Seder table and each can explain the symbolism of the different parts of the meal. If they make sufficient Charoset this could be shared out during the assembly.

Charoset
230g (8 oz) apples;
60g (2 oz) raisins;
60g (2 oz) almonds or walnuts;
a pinch of cinnamon;
a small quantity of sweet wine.

Peel and core the apples. Chop them finely with the nuts and raisins. Add a pinch of cinnamon to taste and then add the wine. Mix together to form a paste.

Holi

Age range
Five to twelve.

Presentation
Teacher and children.

What you need
Coloured streamers made
from crêpe paper.

What to do
Holi is the Hindu Spring Festival of Colour. It celebrates
the love of the god Krishna for a girl called Radha. It
marks the time when the first wheat and barley crops are
harvested and is also a fire festival. It lasts for five days
and is an excuse for everyone to have great fun. People
throw red powder or coloured water over each other and
it is also a time when people are allowed to make fun of
things usually respected. There are usually lively
processions and bonfires are lit. The bonfires symbolise
the burning of last year's rubbish and making a fresh
start. Holi is also a time for visiting friends and relatives
and a chance to make up for any disagreements.

Throwing red paint at each other could be somewhat
hazardous, but the idea can be incorporated in making
'splash paintings', using red paint, for the assembly. The
children could start the assembly with a lively procession
to the accompaniment of Indian music. The children
should wear brightly coloured clothes. They could make
masks to represent characters from Indian folklore and
throw coloured streamers made from crêpe paper at
each other. One group could perform an improvised fire
dance using streamers to represent the flames.

Palm Sunday

Age range
Five to twelve.

Presentation
Teacher and class.

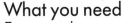

What you need
Easter poles.
Songs 'Lord of the Dance', *SSL*; 'Hurray for Jesus', *SSL*;
'We Have a King Who Rides a Donkey', *SSL*.

What to do
Palm Sunday marks the beginning of Holy Week. It is the day when we remember how Jesus rode into Jerusalem on a donkey. The crowd greeted him by waving palm branches but as these are not to be found in cooler climates it has been traditional to decorate the church and people's houses with evergreen branches of yew, hazel or willow. Arrange for the children to gather some green branches and make some Easter poles for a Palm Sunday procession.

In the assembly the children can dramatise the story of Jesus' entry into Jerusalem. They could then lead all the other children in a procession round the hall whilst singing the songs suggested. In some areas it is traditional to 'Beat the Bounds' at this time of year. This entails defining the boundaries of a parish by making a procession around them and beating the ground with sticks. The children could lead their procession round the perimeter of the school to mark your own bounds.

Easter poles

What you need
A stick; a hoop (not more than 30cm in diameter) formed from a bent metal hanger; strips of old newspaper; crêpe paper and ribbons; stiff coloured card; sweets or raisins.

What to do
First, wrap the newspaper round the hoop, to pad it; finish with layers of crêpe paper. The hoop is then slung from the pole (which is also decorated with crêpe paper): use crêpe paper or ribbons and secure the hoop with a drawing pin at the top of the pole. Each child cuts several shapes from stiff card: bells, flowers, eggs etc, which are decorated and suspended from the hoop. Finally a large chicken shape is cut from yellow card (in Holland, traditionally, this hen is made of baked bread) and secured to the top of the Easter pole. Its eyes are either sweets or raisins.

New light, new life

Age range
Seven to twelve.

Presentation
Teacher.

What you need
Song 'New light, new life', David Self (see below).

New light, new life
Carry a candle to home from church,
Singing a hymn as we walk along:
We're bringing new light and singing a song
    As on Easter morn
    Home we come hymning.

And all the games that we play,
The songs that we sing,
All tell of one thing:
New light, new life, new light, new life!
Everyone's happy on Easter Day!

Hunt in the garden for painted eggs,
Hidden in bushes by Easter Hare:
He puts them all there with cunning and care
    So on Easter's morn
    Out we go hunting.

Wearing new clothes, we're off to the fair,
Rolling our eggs, boiled hard, down the hill:
And sharing dark choc'late, all with goodwill
    As on Easter's morn
    Here we are playing.

David Self

What to do
Discuss with the children why light is useful, how it makes things grow, why some people are frightened of the dark, etc. Can they think of expressions which underline this idea, such as light at the end of the tunnel, throwing light on the subject etc?

Tell the story of how all went dark on Good Friday and how Easter Day dawned brightly. Children are often perplexed by the name Good Friday: explain why it has this name, expand on Jesus' dying for man's sin and the theme of atonement.

Talk about the things that we do to celebrate Easter and how Easter comes at a time of the year when everything is coming to life. Draw the children's attention to the words of the song which capture this association. Mention the festival of Diwali, which also centres around the concept of new light, and link the two festivals together.

Diwali

Age range
Five to twelve.

Presentation
Teacher and class.

What you need
Cardboard candles of all shapes and sizes, decorated with bright crayon patterns, metallic paper, sequins and other decorative materials.
Music 'Rang Rang', Indian classical instrumental music EMI (ECSD 2773) or any other suitable recording of Indian music.
Song 'Diwali is here', *TB*.

What to do
Diwali is the most famous Indian festival celebrated by both Sikhs and Hindus. It takes place in the autumn and is both a new-year festival and a festival of light. Diwali celebrates the return of Rama, the legendary god-king, and his wife Sita to their kingdom after 14 years of exile. They are guided home by thousands of lights lit by the people of their kingdom. Light (believed to drive away the power of darkness and evil) is the major theme of the celebrations.

The children can act out the story of Rama and Sita as part of the assembly. They can also display their model candles; older children could make real candles using wax and dyes of melted down wax crayons. The theme of light can be celebrated with group recitations of selected poems or, better still, poems written by the children themselves.

Advent

Age range
Five to twelve.

Presentation
Teacher.

What you need
Songs 'Let There be Peace on Earth', *ALL*; 'This Little Light of Mine', *ALL*; 'There's a Light That is Shining', *ST*; 'Bring a Light to Shine in Darkness', *NH*; 'Tell Me What Month Was Jesus Born?', *ST*; 'From the Darkness Came Light', *CP*.

What to do
At the beginning of the Christian year, celebrate Advent with a series of candle-lighting assemblies. It might be best to organise these for the end of the school day to enhance the effect of the candle light. Start on the nearest Friday to Advent Sunday and light one candle each week until the end of term. Link readings and hymns to the theme of light and the approach of Christmas. Relate these activities to the other festivals of light that are celebrated at this time of year – Diwali, Hannuka (Chanuka) and St Lucia (the Swedish Festival).

An Advent ring

What you need
Five short candles – four red and one white; a little candle wax; a piece of plywood or chipboard, approximately 30cm square; silver foil; Plasticine; sprigs of evergreen leaves.

What to do
Cover the base with foil and mark a circle, approximately 11 cm radius; mark the centre. Arrange the four red candles equidistant around the circle and secure with a little molten wax. Then secure the white candle on the centre point.

Roll the plasticine into four lengths of approximately 10 cm and fit it around the circle line between the candles. Press into place firmly. Decorate with sprigs evergreen.

An Advent calendar

What you need
Empty cardboard boxes of various sizes; white paint; coloured tissue paper; black paper; a Stanley knife and a small electric lamp.

What to do
Select a box sufficiently large for the lamp to fit inside without danger of burning the sides. Glue other boxes round the sides. Cut holes in the adjoining walls so light can pass through.

Using the Stanley knife, (teacher only!) cut out 24 windows – including one for the stable. Paint the outside of the boxes white. Then using coloured tissue paper, make stained-glass windows to stick behind the openings. On the stable opening stick black paper silhouettes.

Cover each of the windows with black paper shutters made to fit, and number these from 1 to 24. Switch on the lamp. Let them open one window for each day of Advent.

Happy Christmas

Age range
Five to eight.

Presentation
Teacher and class.

What you need
Sheets of card 30 cm × 20 cm; copies of the support material on page 121.
Song 'We Wish You A Merry Christmas'.

What to do
In preparation for the assembly the children write out the letters that spell Happy Christmas singly on the sheets of card. Colour these boldly so that they can be seen clearly round the hall. Next the children think of as many items as they can linked to Christmas and the nativity story, beginning with the appropriate letters. They can then illustrate the items on the same-sized cards to carry in alongside the letters. Here are a few suggestions – they will be able to think of a lot more.

H – Holy Family
A – Angels
P – Puddings/prayers/parties
P – Presents/parcels
Y – Yule log/yew tree

C – Candles/cards/crackers/cakes/carols
H – Holly/happiness/holy/halo
R – Robins/reindeer
I – Ice/icing on cake/innkeeper/ivy
S – Santa/St Nicholas/sleigh bells
T – Turkey/tree
M – Mary/Magi/mistletoe
A – Advent
S – Shepherds/star/stable/singing.

Christmas around the world

Age range
Seven to twelve.

Presentation
Several classes.

What you need
Information on Christmas customs around the world. *The Christmas Book*, Macdonald Educational; *The Christmas Book*, Esme Eve, Chatto & Windus; *The Oxford Christmas Book for Children*, OUP.
Carols Calypso carol, *YP*; Cowboy carol, *MB*.
Music 'Child for the World' (The Spinners on record).

What to do
Children love to know how Christmas is celebrated around the world. Allocate a different country to each class group and make the final assembly a culmination of this project.

Describe how a female Santa, La Befana, is celebrated in Italy. A kind witch, she fills the stockings of good children on January 6 but there's the threat that she might eat the naughty ones. Many European countries still distribute Christmas gifts on the eve of St Nicholas' Day, 6 December. In Holland they re-enact the legendary arrival of St Nicholas by boat from Spain, accompanied by his Moorish attendant, Black Peter. He carries a sack full of presents for the good children (and a stick to beat the wicked).

Explain the Mexican custom of *las posadas* and allow the children involved in the assembly to make and play with a *piñata*. This is a colourfully decorated papier mâché container filled with sweets and small toys and hung on a string. Children take turns to leap up and hit it in order to dislodge the contents.

Reproducible material

Bookworms, see page 12

The Bookworms have read

_____

We think it is

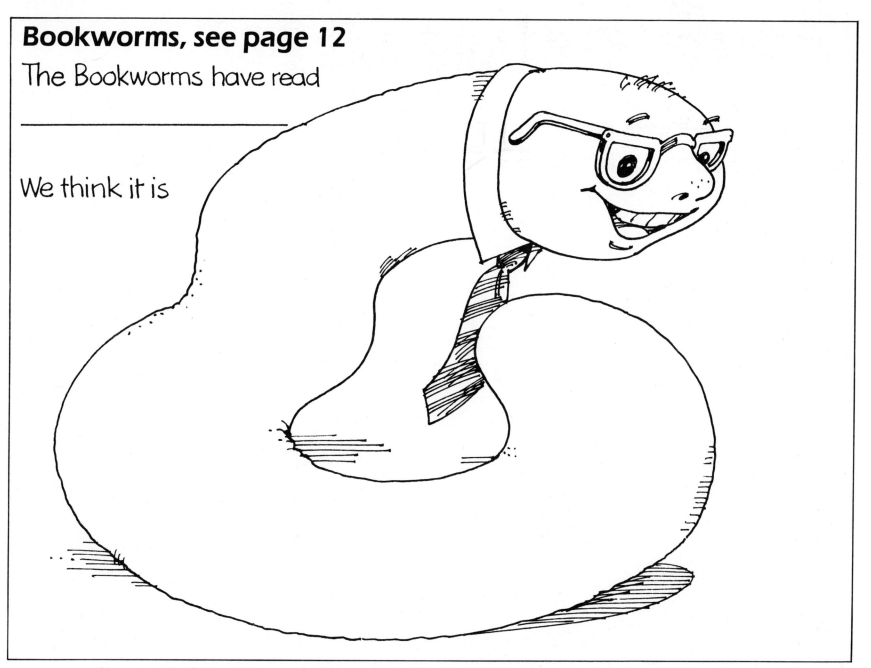

FEELINGS

1. Happy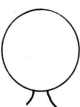

2. Sad

3. Angry

4. Sorry

Draw in the
face and then
the body to show
a person who is —

5. Frightened

6. Proud

7. Ashamed

8. Surprised

Super people, see page 37

THE DAILY NEWS

PRICE 20p

TUESDAY 8th SEPTEMBER

SUPER

SAVES THE DAY

I Spy, see page 59

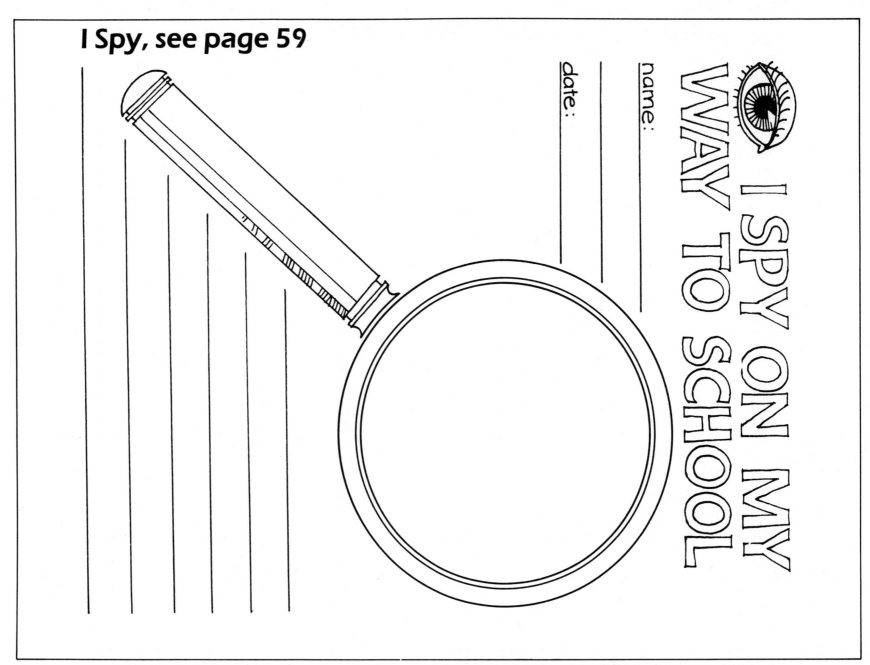

I SPY ON MY
WAY TO SCHOOL

name:

date:

Happy Christmas, see page 114

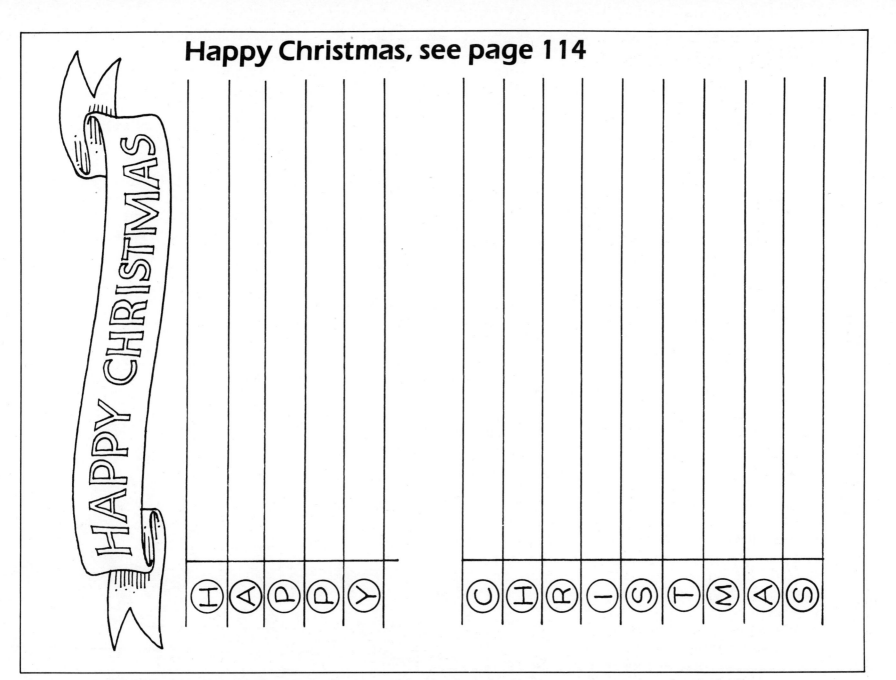

Assemblies calendar

January
1 New Year's Day.
6 Epiphany (Christian), when the Three Wise Men are said to have discovered the child Jesus.
6 Twelfth Night.
7 Christmas Day for some Eastern Orthodox Christians.
● Chinese New Year Festival.

February
2 Candlemas (Christian).
14 St Valentine's Day (Christian).
● Shrove Tuesday (Christian).
● Ash Wednesday (Christian), the start of Lent.
● Lent, when Christians pray and fast.
● Purim (Jewish) celebrates the deliverance of the Jews from Persia by Esther.

March
1 St David's Day, Patron of Wales (Christian).
17 St Patrick's Day, Patron of Ireland (Christian).
20 First day of Spring.
● Mothering Sunday, the fourth Sunday in Lent.
● Pesach or Passover (Jewish), celebrating the deliverance of the Jews from slavery in Egypt by Moses.

● Holi (Hindi) the five-day spring festival which celebrates the love of Krishna and Radha.
● Holy Week (Christian), the week leading up to and including Easter Sunday, when Christ's suffering, death and resurrection are remembered.

April
1 All Fool's Day.
4 Martin Luther King assassinated.
4/5 Ch'ing Ming, the Chinese festival of Pure Brightness, when graves are visited and ancestors remembered.
13 Baisakhi, the Hindu and Sikh festival marking the religious New Year.
23 St George's Day, Patron Saint of England (Christian).

May
1 May Day festivals mark the end of winter and the beginning of spring.
● Wesak or Full Moon Day, when Theravada Buddhists celebrate the birth of Siddhartha Gautama, their founder.
● Ascension Day (Christian), commemorating the day Jesus rose into heaven.
● Whitsun (Christian), celebrating the day the Holy Spirit descended on the disciples.
● Shavuoth or Pentecost, the Jewish spring festival which marks the time that God gave Moses the Ten Commandments on Sinai.

June
21 Summer Solstice and the longest day.
24 Midsummer Day.
● Fathers' Day.
● World Children's Day.

July
15 St Swithin's Day
● Chinese Festival of Maidens.

August

15 Assumption of Blessed Virgin Mary (Roman Catholic).
- Janmashtami (Hindi), celebrating the birth of the god Krishna.
- Anniversary of the Guru Granth Sahib, holy scriptures of the Sikhs.
- Raksha Bandhan, a festival for Hindu sisters and brothers.
- Yue Lan, the Chinese feast of Hungry Ghosts.

September

- Rosh Hashanah (Jewish), the New Year.
- Yom Kippur (Jewish), the Day of Atonement.
- Succoth or Sukkat (Jewish), the harvest festival.
- Chung Ch'iu, the Chinese feast of the moon goddess.
- Durga Puja (Hindi).

October

31 All Hallows Eve or Hallowe'en.
- Autumn harvest festival (Christian).
- Diwali, the Indian new year festival when Hindus celebrate the reunion of Rama with Sita and the Sikhs celebrate the building of the Golden Temple of Amritsar.

November

1 All Saints' Day.
5 Guy Fawkes Night (UK).
30 St Andrew's Day, Patron Saint of Scotland.
- Advent Sunday (Christian).

December

6 St Nicholas Day (Christian), remembering the first Santa Claus.
8 Bodhi Day (Buddhist) celebrating Siddhartha Gautama becoming the first Buddha.
8 Immaculate Conception of the Blessed Virgin Mary (Roman Catholic).
24 Christmas Eve (Christian).
25 Christmas Day (Christian).
26 Boxing Day and the Feast of St Stephen.
31 New Year's Eve and Hogmanay.
- Birthday of Guru Gobind Singh (Sikh).
- Chanukah or Hannukah (Jewish), the Festival of Light.

Islamic festivals

These fall on different days each year because they follow the cycle of the moon.
- Ramadan (Muslim), a fast from sunrise to sunset which lasts from one new moon to the next.
- Eid-ul-Fitr, the celebration of the end of Ramadan.
- Eid-ul-Adha, the celebration of the Abraham and Isaac story.
- Lailat-ul-Bara'h (Muslim), the Night of Forgiveness.

Useful addresses

Animal Welfare Trust
Tylers Way
Watford By-Pass
Watford
Herts WD2 8HG

Band Aid
PO Box 4TX
London W1A 4TX

Buddhist Society
58 Eccleston Square
London SW1V 1PH

Centre for World Development
  Education
Regent's College
Inner Circle
Regent's Park
London NW1 4NS

Christian Aid
240–250 Ferndale Road
Brixton
London SW9 8BH

Commission for Racial Equality
Elliot House
10–12 Allington Street
London SW1E 5EH

Commonwealth Institute
Kensington High Street
London W8

Dr Barnardo's Homes
Tanner's Lane
Barkingside
Ilford
Essex IG6 1QG

The Flora and Fauna Preservation
  Society
c/o Zoological Society of London
Regent's Park
London NW1 4RY

Friends of the Earth Ltd
377 City Road
London EC1V 1MA

The Health Education Council
78 New Oxford Street
London WC1A 1AH

The Hindu Centre
39 Grafton Terrace
off Malden Street
London NW5 4JA

Inner London Education Authority
School Equipment Centre
275 Kennington Lane
London SE11

International Boys' Town Trust
50 Willesden Avenue
Walton
Peterborough PE4 6EA

Islamic Cultural Centre
146 Park Road
London NW8

The Jewish National Fund
Harold Poster House
Kingsbury Circle
London NW9

Muslim Welfare House and
  Information Services
233 Seven Sisters Road
London N4 2DA

National Centre for Alternative
  Technology
Llwyngwern Quarry
Machynlleth
Powys SY20 9AZ

National Children's Homes
85 Highbury Park
London N5

National Trust
Education Adviser
8 Church Street
Lacock
Wiltshire SN15 2LB

The Otter Trust
Earsham
Near Bungay
Suffolk

Oxfam
Effra Development Education Unit
Effra School
Barnwell Road
London SW2 1PL

Paraplegic Games Director-General
International Stoke Mandeville
   Games Federation
Ludwig Guttman Sports Centre for
   the Disabled
Harvey Road
Aylesbury
Buckinghamshire HP21 8PP

Play for Life
31b Ipswich Road
Norwich
Norfolk NR2 2LN

British Red Cross Society
9 Grosvenor Crescent
London SW1X 7EJ

Royal National Institute for the Blind
224 Great Portland Street
London W1N 6AA

Royal National Institute for the Deaf
105 Gower Street
London WC1E 6AH

Royal National Lifeboat Institute
West Quay Road
Poole
Dorset BH15 1HZ

Royal Society for the Prevention of
   Accidents (RoSPA)
Cannon House
The Priory
Queensway
Birmingham B4 6BS

Royal Society for the Prevention of
   Cruelty to Animals
The Causeway
Horsham
West Sussex RH12 1HG

Royal Society for the Protection of
   Birds
The Lodge
Sandy
Bedfordshire SG19 2DL

Save the Children Fund
Mary Datchelor House
17 Grove Lane
London SE5 8RD

The Sikh Cultural Society
88 Mollison Way
Edgware
Middlesex HA8 5QW

Swan Rescue Service
Lathe Green Farm House
Shotesham St Mary
Norwich
Norfolk

United Nations Children's Fund
   (UNICEF)
55 Lincoln's Inn Fields
London WC2A 3NB

Wildlife Youth Service
Marston Court
98–106 Manor Road
Wallington
Surrey

The World Wildlife Fund
11–13 Ockford Road
Godalming
Surrey GU7 1QU

War on Want
1 London Bridge Street
London SE1

Keys to song books and prayer books

Key to song books

ALL	Alleluya, A & C Black
AP	Apusskidu, A & C Black
CP	Come and Praise, BBC
ECS	Every Colour Under the Sun, Ward Lock
GY	Granny's Yard, Bell & Hyman
HQ	Harlequin, A & C Black
LBHS	The Ladybird Book of Hymns and Songs, Ladybird
MB	Merrily to Bethlehem, A & C Black
MCF	Musical Calendar of Festivals, Ward Lock
NCS	New Child Songs, NCEC
NH	New Horizon, Stainer & Bell
NO	New Orbit, Stainer & Bell
NW	New World, Oxford University Press
OK	Okk-tokki-unga, A & C Black
SAS	Sing a Song, Nelson
SSL	Someone's Singing Lord, A & C Black
SLW	Sound of Living Water, Hodder & Stoughton
ST	Sing True, Religious Education Press
TA	Ta-ra-ra-boom-de-ay, A & C Black
TB	Tinderbox, A & C Black
YP	Youth Praise, Falcon

Key to prayer books

CPAW	Children's Prayers from Around the World, Lion
HMP	Home-made Prayers, Lion
LPT	Let's Pray Together, Collins
LBCP	The Lion Book of Children's Prayers, Lion
LBFP	The Lion Book of Famous Prayers, Lion
TWI	Together with Infants, Roberts Fisher, Evans, 1982
TAP	Themes and Prayers, Margaret Ovens, Macmillan Educational, 1974
WYP	When You Pray with 7–10s, NCEC

Acknowledgements

The author and publisher extend grateful thanks for the reuse of material first published in *Hands Together* to: W Owen Cole for 'Texts from world religions'; Sue Humphries for 'The cycle of life'; Fiona Shore for 'It's tasty', 'This is your life', 'Chinese New Year', 'Patience is a virtue', 'Turning the other cheek'; Cheryl M Elkins for 'The growth of inequality'; Sandra Kerr for the poem 'Supermum'; Geoffrey Curtis for the story 'In the beginning'; David Self for 'Turning the other cheek', the song 'New light, new life' and details of Mary Seacole and Corrie ten Boom; Jenny Nemko for 'The family of man and woman'; Julie Grove for the rewritten version of 'The story of Mahagri'; Geoffrey Marshall Taylor for 'The signs of Sikhism' and 'Signs around us'; John Snelling for the stories 'The wounded swan' and 'The mouse and the crow or How enemies became friends'; and Robert Lamb for the story 'Moving on'; Bob Docherty for 'You are what you eat' and 'Famine'.

The publishers also gratefully acknowledge permission to reproduce material from the following sources:

Blackie & Sons Ltd for 'Dreamtime' (originally published as the 'Creation story' from *Worlds of Difference*, Martin Palmer and Esther Bissett; Puffin Books Ltd for 'Supply teacher' from *Please Mrs Butler* by Allan Ahlberg; UNICEF, New York for the following games: 'The fish spear', 'Fire on the mountain', 'Clap ball' and 'Networks'; John and the Adult Education Council, Norwich for the quote from *The Opening Door*; 'Mix the pancake' by Christina Rossetti.

Our thanks to Pictorial Charts Educational Trust, 27 Kirchen Road, West Ealing, London W13 0UD for supplying the references for the five Ks of Sikhism (page 86) in their Sikh festivals chart set, available at £4.00 plus 60p VAT per set.

Every effort has been made to trace and acknowledge contributors. If any right has been omitted the publishers offer their apologies and will rectify this in subsequent editions following publication.

Other Scholastic books

Bright Ideas
The *Bright Ideas* books provide a wealth of resources for busy primary school teachers. There are now more than 20 titles published, providing clearly explained and illustrated ideas on topics ranging from *Writing* and *Maths Activities* to *Assemblies* and *Christmas Art and Craft*. Each book contains material which can be photocopied for use in the classroom.

Teacher Handbooks
The *Teacher Handbooks* give an overview of the latest research in primary education, and show how it can be put into practice in the classroom. Covering all the core areas of the curriculum, the *Teacher Handbooks* are indispensable to the new teacher as a source of information and useful to the experienced teacher as a quick reference guide.

Management Books
The *Management Books* are designed to help teachers to organise their time, classroom and teaching more efficiently. The books deal with topical issues, such as *Parents and Schools* and organising and planning *Project Teaching*, and are written by authors with lots of practical advice and experiences to share.

Let's Investigate
Let's Investigate is an exciting range of photocopiable maths activity books giving open-ended investigative tasks. The series will complement and extend any existing maths programme. Designed to cover the 6 to 12-year-old age range these books are ideal for small group or individual work. Each book presents progressively more difficult concepts and many of the activities can be adapted for use throughout the primary school. Detailed teacher's notes outlining the objectives of each photocopiable sheet and suggesting follow-up activities have been included.